Evangelicals and Liberation

CARL E. ARMERDING, *Editor*

Studies in the World Church and Missions

HARVIE M. CONN, *Editor*

EVANGELICALS
AND
LIBERATION

HARVIE M. CONN　　　　**STEPHEN C. KNAPP**
KENNETH HAMILTON　　**CLARK H. PINNOCK**

Edited by
CARL E. ARMERDING

PRESBYTERIAN AND REFORMED PUBLISHING CO.
PHILLIPSBURG, NEW JERSEY
1979

Table of Contents

Introduction

In April, 1976, at the invitation of President Kenneth G. Hanna and the Evangelical Theological Society of Canada, the papers included in this volume were presented to the Annual Conference under the theme, "The Theology of Liberation." It is indicative of a growing maturity within the society that, for the first time, theologians from across Canada and beyond were assembled to address a common theme; in this case a theme of vital interest to the community of Christian thought both within and outside the geographical limits of Canada itself. It is also to the credit of the society's leaders that no attempt was made to produce a uniform or doctrinaire approach to the subject, as the following contributions will make abundantly clear. What was then, and happily remains now, the concern of the society is that the Word of God be allowed to speak and that the evangelical gospel as the only fountainhead and source of true liberation be clearly affirmed. In this common commitment all of the contributors share.

To that end, contributions were sought from theologians of varied sub-disciplines and professional and ecclesiastical backgrounds. Senior to the group is Professor Kenneth Hamilton of the University of Winnipeg, whose role as an important theological interpreter within the United Church of Canada gave a valuable dimension to the conference. His perspicacious critique of fuzzy thinking, in whatever guise it appears, clarified issues and challenged the conferees to a rigorous submission to Scripture and plain, clear logic. Another two papers come from the able pen of Dr. Harvie M. Conn, Professor of Missions and Apologetics at Westminster Theological Seminary in Philadelphia, U.S.A. Dr. Conn's experience on the mission field as

vii

well as in the classroom, combined with a fervent rejection of any truncated gospel, made his ministry to the conference a unique challenge. His addresses, more than any others, took the conferees away from the North American scene to consider a liberation that truly represents good news to the Third World poor as well as the Western world rich.

The centrality of the "Exodus" theme for liberation, particularly in its Latin American dress, provided occasion for the editor's (Professor of O.T., Regent College, Vancouver) examination of scriptural bases for the new theology, with special reference to hermeneutical method. This paper, in slightly revised form, was also presented as the 1976 Presidential Address to the North-West Region, American Academy of Religion/Society of Biblical Literature, in May, 1976, in Eugene, Oregon. And finally, the conference considered a ringing call to self-liberation from the oppression of our North American materialism and the slavery of consumerism. Dr. Clark H. Pinnock, Professor of Theology at Regent College, Vancouver, left no doubt in anyone's mind that our examination of liberation theology and liberation movements remains hollow apart from a new willingness to look at those structures which have oppressed our society and, through us, the rest of the world.

A seventh paper, though not given at the conference itself, was added to the collection as an appropriate supplement to the discussions in Toronto. Originally prepared for a dialogue between United Methodists and Evangelicals in Washington, D.C., this essay came from the pen of Stephen C. Knapp of the Philadelphia-based Partnership in Mission organization. Addressing the important question of theological method, Mr. Knapp's critique of Gutiérrez' *A Theology of Liberation* stands as a valuable challenge to the common methodology of much Third World thought.

Conferees in Toronto showed by their varied and concise responses to the papers (the inclusion of which, had it been practical, would have considerably enriched this volume) an interest in the subject far exceeding the merely academic. No doubt each of the chapters could have been strengthened by revision in light of the discussion, but the concern of the conference that contemporaneity take precedence over polish has been honored. Each of the papers set forth is published exactly as given, apart from minor changes in style. As editor, I should like to thank each contributor for his immediate consent to this request, especially so as none of the papers were written with publication in view. We ask only that our readers judge our efforts in light of that fact.

Our shared concern is that the Word of God shall be given free course in the church of Jesus Christ. The Word of God and the testimony of Jesus require us to think in terms of human liberation. It is evident to many of us that the implications of the subject have not been allowed to sink deep into our evangelical consciousness, and we acknowledge our dept to all who have broadened our horizons, even those of whose thinking and methodology we are critical. It is our hope that not only evangelicals but those whose Christian commitment has found expression within other groups will read and ponder the message of these essays. Our affirmation of the evangelical faith is made in the conviction that this faith represents in broadest terms the teaching of Scriptures. In this we hope to remain open to correction, especially as it embodies new insights from the Scriptures, which authority we accept as total and complete in these matters. If the papers here presented help in any way to a more complete understanding of the Word of God and its implications for the church in the world of today, our labors shall not have been in vain.

I should like, also, to thank Mr. Charles Craig and the Presbyterian and Reformed Publishing Company for their willingness to undertake speedy publication of this volume. In today's competitive publishing world, their commitment to serving the Christian community stands as a model. Finally, a word of appreciation is due Dr. Harvie Conn for handling certain details which would normally have been the work of the editor. His energy and efficiency continue to be an inspiration and challenge to those with whom he works.

CARL EDWIN ARMERDING
Regent College
Vancouver, British Columbia
October, 1976

I. Liberation Theology: An Overview

KENNETH HAMILTON*

Theological movements have succeeded one another—one might almost say have tumbled over one another—since the end of World War II. Most of these have been short-lived, and some of these have been trivial. Liberation theology, on the other hand, seems likely to remain on the scene for some time to come. It has a solidity and a breadth of appeal that most of its predecessors lacked. Its adoption by the World Council of Churches—first in Bankok in 1972 and then in Nairobi in 1975—has added to its prestige and given its tenets wide publicity. For this theology is not simply one to tickle the palates of jaded intellectuals eager to sample the flavor of a new mix of esoteric concepts. It has an appeal reaching beyond the circles of academia and ecclesia. Its name sounds quite familiar to the general public that hears every day about Women's Liberation, Black Liberation, Gay Liberation, and so on.

Liberation theology has two sides: a practical and a theoretical. The two sides are interconnected, yet also separable. While the theoretical side has drawn its inspiration and maintains its missionary fervor from the careers of revolutionary churchmen in the Third World—particularly in Latin America—it also has developed its ideas in the study, quite remote from involvement in a revolutionary situation. North Americans and Europeans may indeed read such Latin American authors as Rubem Alves or Gustavo Gutiérrez, but they are

---

* Kenneth Hamilton, Ph.D., is Associate Professor of Systematic Theology at United College, an institution of the United Church of Canada in Winnipeg, Manitoba. The first Protestant theologian to author a book-length assessment of Paul Tillich's system of philosophical theology, he has also analyzed contemporary theology in such works as *Revolt Against Heaven* and *God Is Dead*. With his wife, he has also co-authored a number of titles evaluating modern literature.

1

most likely to digest liberation theology through books by Jürgen Moltmann, Dorothee Soelle, Harvey Cox, Rosemary Ruether, and John Pairman Brown. It is the theoretical side that will be my concern in this chapter. In my second chapter I shall try to draw together to some extent the two sides.

I

Chronologically, liberation theology followed the theology of hope; and the theology of hope followed the theology of the death of God. I believe that, looking back, we can see that this was no arbitrary sequence. The progression has been the clarification of a concept of the relation between God and the world departing drastically from the traditional Christian understanding of that relation.

Theologians of the death of God proclaimed that they were advocating a "radical" or "revolutionary" Christianity. In this they were correct, although the language which they used made so little contact with that of the man-on-the-street that their claim made little impression. Once the shock-value of their slogan, "God has died—in our time, in our generation," had been exhausted, the negativity of their message defeated them. The death of God was taken as a joke rather than as a revelation. "Our God is alive. Sorry about Yours." This sentence on a church bulletin board summarized the most common reaction.

Nevertheless, the death-of-God theologians were making a serious point, though they never found a common, intelligible language in which to present it. They were arguing that a God conceived in independence from the world of human consciousness and ruling over his creation was a concept to be discarded. The God directing human history was incredible after Auschwitz, said Richard Rubenstein. Karl Barth's God who speaks his Word from heaven was irrelevant to people inspired by the Kennedy fervor, the gaity of the Beatles' songs, and the expectations of the Freedom marchers, said William Hamilton. Thomas Altizer (the most theoretically minded of the group) taught that we must rediscover Hegel's vision of a God no

2

longer transcendent over the world but revealing himself through the secular experience of the process of change in human history. A return to Hegel's vision of God revealed in the process of world history and becoming self-conscious in human consciousness was, in fact, the real focus of "radical" theology as the death-of-God theologians sensed it and were trying to explain it. Quite a while earlier, Martin Buber in his book, *The Eclipse of God,* had argued that our modern consciousness is by no means averse to religion but is resistant to faith—that is, to belief in a God who is real in himself and is not to be identified with human consciousness but who *addresses* man. The accuracy of Buber's estimate was to be seen in the welcome given to Bishop Robinson's *Honest to God.* There Robinson attacked the concept of a God "up there" or "out there," without making clear just what he would put in his place. Robinson certainly caught a popular mood, and his vagueness enabled him to be heard by many Christians who were not yet prepared to attack traditional Christianity directly and who yet had subconsciously rejected "faith" in the sense indicated by Buber. Robinson expressed his conviction that in *Honest to God* he had erred in not being radical enough. His "soft radicalism" (as William Hamilton termed it) was soon taken up in the hard radicalism of the death-of-God theologians. This hard radicalism, however, could have no widespread appeal so long as it was tied to a negative proclamation that did not relate itself in an obvious manner to twentieth-century ideals and expectations. The death-of-God theologians argued in vain that their message was essentially one of hopefulness and liberation. But virtually the same message *was* warmly received when it was proclaimed under the title of the theology of hope.

The ghost of Hegel—so specifically invoked by Altizer—is the unseen presence at the banquet to which we are invited by the theologians of hope. In his book, *Origins of the Theology of Hope,* M. Douglas Meeks, while consistently underplaying the Hegelian elements in Moltmann's thinking, admits that Moltmann became convinced of the necessity of "doing theology" in the context of Hegel's understanding of the death of God experienced in "the openness of history and the totality of experience." It is noteworthy that Moltmann introduces his final remarks in his *Theology of Hope* by quoting Hegel's dialectical theory: "A thing is alive only when it contains contradiction in itself and is indeed the power of holding the contradiction within itself and enduring it." It is this human capability, says Moltmann, that gives to our lives meaning, freedom, and the capacity for handling creatively "events and processes which are open towards the future of God."

The *future of God* of which Moltmann speaks is not at all merely the future *ordained by God,* but is (in Hegelian fashion) the future to which God himself is moving. The theology of hope denies that possibility of anchoring ourselves in faith concerning what God has already done for the world in the death and resurrection of Jesus. It points to hope in the "not yet" of the future of God as the ground of our present believing.

II

Liberation theology and the theology of hope are one and the same in their foundation. (Moltmann went on to write *The Gospel of Liberation* and Rubem Alves calls his book on liberation theology *A Theology of Human Hope.*) But they are not identical. While the ghost of Hegel presides over the theology of hope, the spiritual begetters of the theology of liberation are the Young Hegelians. The Young Hegelians accepted Hegel's dialectic of life as the tension between contradictions. But they changed the focus of Hegel's vision of world history. For them it was not enough to understand the unfolding process, since the crunch came with our present participation in it. As Karl Marx's famous statement puts it, "Hitherto philosophers have explained the world; our task is to change it." Atheism was the general stance of the Young Hegelians, because the death of God made plain for them that the function of guiding history which had previously been imagined to belong to divinity was now unequivocally the responsibility of humanity. The pain of the contradictions felt within all life was being manifest in the human experience of alienation. To overcome all alienation was the goal of the world

4

process; and so an alienated God (the divine separated from the human and set above it) was the first alienation to be overcome. Again, as Marx put it, "The criticism of religion is the premise of all criticism."

The Young Hegelians, too, adopted Hegel's view that all social reality arises out of the master-slave contradiction. Thus they assumed that all social action must be directed to overcoming the oppression/liberation polarity. For Marx this meant that class warfare is the sole means of struggling to the goal to which world history is directed; and therefore that revolution is the instrument essential to reaching it at last. The goal, moreover, is literally utopian. Utopia is "no place"; and history's liberated culmination is now not to be found. It is not; for it is hidden in the "not yet."

Liberation theology takes both its basic premise (the oppression/liberation polarity) and its basic strategy (the belief that salvation can come only through the revoltionary action of the oppressed) from the Young Hegelians. As Gutiérrez has asserted, liberation theology conceives of history "as a process of the liberation of man." He writes,

> The goal is not only better living conditions, a radical change of structures, a social revolution; it is much more: the continuous creation, never ending, of a new way to be a man, *a permanent cultural revolution.*

And he speaks of Utopia as an "annunciation" of what is not yet but will be—"a pro-jection into the future, a dynamic and mobilizing factor in history."

With the relative stagnation of revolutionary fervor in Marxist Russia today, Young Hegelianism is once more, as it was in the eighteen-forties, an active creed. Two recent incarnations of the Young Hegelian spirit have been influential in molding the doctrines of liberation theology: Herbert Marcuse and Ernst Bloch. Both champion the young Marx as opposed to the Marx who has become embalmed in Leninist-Marxist orthodoxy. Bloch, in particular, has been taken up as an oracle by Jurgen Moltmann, because of Bloch's positive reading of religion as the vehicle by means of which the hope-principle has been communicated in history. Marx, so Bloch com-

5

plains, failed to see the role which theology has played in bringing about Utopia by insisting that history is open-ended for human purposes and that it will find its perfection in the coming universal kingdom of God. Bloch writes, "The meaning of human history already from the start is the building of the commonwealth of freedom." He also says, "All that is not *hope,* is wooden, dead, hampering, as ponderous and awkward as the word reality. There is no freedom, but only imprisonment."

III

It is of more than casual significance that Bloch values in the Bible above all else the statement of the serpent in Eden, "Ye shall be as gods." In this, Bloch follows Hegel. For Hegel, man's disobedience is the necessary precondition of his entry into responsible, creative living and so into godlikeness. Liberation theology, to be consistent, must follow Bloch in his dislike of the word "reality" and in his belief that obedience to the Creator is submission to the oppression of the alien God. If the basic truth about the human condition is the master-slave relation in which the slave must choose between oppression and liberation, then the archetypal Master is the Creator God, and the source of all the "dehumanizing structures" standing in the way of human liberation lies in the will of the Creator. It is this God who must die in order that a free humanity may live.

Once salvation is identified with liberation from every oppressive structure, reality (that which *is*) becomes viewed as the sphere of evil which is destined to be overthrown to that which is to be—the future of God that brings with it the coming Utopia. The Saviour or Christ of the liberated future is the spirit of humanity awakened to combat the repressive structures ordained and sustained by the Creator God. Conscious that the power of the old alienated God has passed away with its own awakening, humanity perceives itself to be the carrier of the future of God, the true divinity of the next age. Its saving task, then, is to bring about (in Gutiérrez' words) "the continuous creation, never ending, of a new way to be a man."

6

A new way to be a man has arrived, because man has liberated the divinity within him and thus has created himself anew. This new creation is continuous, because the liberated spirit knows no end except Utopia—which is *no place* but an infinite prospect. That the Christ of the liberation outlook is humanity (and that Jesus the Liberator is at most the Morning Star of the liberated Dawn) is clear from the way in which those who proclaim the gospel of liberation speak of the idea of Utopia as an "annunciation." History is to bear the Christ in the new age when the future of God is revealed in all its glory. Most revealingly, *annunciation* is linked with *denunciation*. The convert to liberationism has to denounce the alienated God and all his works in order to show that he is genuinely committed to the future of God. For the God being formed in the womb of humanity is a jealous God who will not share his godhead with any other. Moreover, the convert has to school himself in *conscientization,* that is, the conscious removal from within himself of all vestiges of "the oppressive consciousness which remain in him." These terms (invented by Paulo Freire) show how liberationism forges new theological terms for its new gospel. Denunciation takes the place of repentance; annunciation of the confession of faith; and conscientization of sanctification.

Since liberationism's God is a "not yet" God, however, the spiritual warfare to which its followers are called lies right at the heart of its message. In the present moment denunciation of the oppressors rather than celebration of the freedom still to be won must be the first sign of the true believer. Equally important (because foundational to the faith) is the recognition that the followers of the alien God must be identified and destroyed before the new gospel can become the effective agent of the new creation. Since it is the very nature of the tares to choke out the good grain, there can be no question of both growing together until the harvest. Now is the time to pull up the tares and cast them into the oven! In respect of the necessity for liberationism's warfare being a violent one, Marcuse's argument has become a classic one. Since an oppressive society (so he argues) is already using violence in the structures of its oppression, it follows that counterviolence is really non-violent because it seeks the removal of these structures and the end of all oppression. In theological terms of a traditional kind, we must sin that grace may abound. Only, liberationists would deny that rebellion against law can ever be called sinful. Oppressive human laws simply mirror the Tyrant Lawgiver who presided over creation, the alien God who must be rooted out of the heart of the liberated individual.

IV

What I have presented so far is the basic structure of liberationist thinking. When one starts by making all his thinking revolve around the oppression/liberation polarity, then the features of the "theology" which I have outlined inevitably emerge. Individual theologians of liberation, of course, do not follow all the implications of their starting-point to their logical conclusion. For example, few books on liberation theology make a clear distinction between the Creator God and the God emerging in liberated humanity. Most endeavor to show Jesus Christ as the unique Liberator and wish to make our attitude to him determinative of our vision of the coming Utopia. Christian liberationists, too, mostly draw back from making the liquidation of the oppressors a necessary condition for entering the first phase of liberated life; and they regard violence to be at most permissible as a last resort rather than seeing it as the norm and a mark of spiritual sincerity.

Yet, even in its best representatives, liberation theology is beset with the dualistic, perfectionistic dogmatisms which I have outlined. I have not touched on its tendentious presentation of "eschatology," a term which it tries to stretch to cover its belief in a new gospel proclaiming the future of God. And I have not spoken of its attempt to show that its new God within humanity can be identified with the God of the Exodus and of the resurrection. Other chapters, I am sure, are covering these areas. There is not time to look at individual thinkers in the movement and show (which would be easy to do) how they at times converge upon the themes treated in these chapters

8

and at times diverge and come close to the traditional Christian understanding of the liberty which is in Christ.

What I have hoped to do is to indicate that liberation theology and kindred theologies (the theology of hope, political theology, and so on) that seek to "concretize" salvation, as their jargon terms it, are offering another salvation from the one spoken of in the Bible because they proclaim another God than the God and Father of our Lord Jesus Christ.

2. A Preliminary Dialogue with Gutiérrez' *A Theology of Liberation*

Introduction

Needless to say, engaging in a critical reflection of the kind to be included in this chapter or, for that matter, entering the kind of dialogue for which this essay was originally prepared, are tasks undertaken in the face of many risks and difficulties.

Hugo Assmann has warned us against making the "theology of liberation" a "consumer product."[1] This chapter and our dialogue certainly run the risk of that. We should enter the process only with a deep resolve not to be merely riding "piggyback" on the radical commitment and reflection of people in the face of injustice in distant places.[2] By way of contrast, this reflection and our dialogue can find justification only to the extent that the fruit of Fr. Gutiérrez' reflection (now available to us in a nice "package" isolated from Latin American reality) can somehow serve as an instrument in the refinement of our own commitment to the gospel and all that this requires in terms of our commitment to those suffering from injustice, whether close to home or far away.[3] This latter expression of concern runs the high risk, of course, of paying lip-service only to an abstract ideal which, for most of us (and certainly for the author) is far beyond what we can yet confess out of actual experience.

Another risk is the concession the form of this reflection (and

---

* Stephen C. Knapp, Th.M., after graduation from Houghton College, pursued theological studies at Westminster Theological Seminary and Princeton Theological Seminary, where he earned his Th.M. in 1969. Since 1968 he has worked as a staff member of Partnership in Mission, Abington, Pa. His chapter was originally presented as a paper at a dialogue between United Methodists and representatives of "Evangelicals for Social Action" in Washington, D. C., July 8-9, 1975.

our dialogue) will undoubtedly make to a theory of knowledge which, thanks to Paulo Freire, we are beginning to see as mistaken, at least, and probably an impediment to a true obedience to Christ. Perhaps all of us are so interested in making a contribution, keeping up with the trends, establishing ourselves as theologians or being involved in meeting with people we regard as important that we are willing in the final analysis to make such concessions. Or perhaps we are just not far enough along in our thinking or in the emergence of the new pedagogy to be able to construct a form of reflection consistent with the intuitions Freire is awakening within us.[4]

Perhaps the greatest risk of all in an essay written by a North American or a discussion among predominantly North Americans on the "theology of liberation" is the risk of paternalism and imperialism.[5] The risks of this are especially high for someone speaking out of a conservative-evangelical background. In this tradition (which is a part of me) the reflex to defend the faith is so often more automatic than the reflex to live the faith—a distortion which seems out of keeping with the very faith we display such an interest in defending! And alongside this, the community incarnating this tradition seems to be perpetually receptive to "pat answers" and acquisitive of an arsenal of weapons with which to oppose emerging heresies—often dehumanizing the "heretic" and shutting off creative theological reflection by Third World theologians within the community in the process.

If this chapter makes it into the growing body of material giving pros and cons on the "theology of liberation," I would hope that it be regarded as a very personal and provisional attempt aimed at the clarification of my own confession in the midst of a still incomplete pilgrimage from fundamentalism to a more biblical and social Christianity. I have little interest in either attempting to correct theological errors of Gutiérrez or aiding other evangelicals (and especially Third World evangelicals) in such an attempt. Gutiérrez and the reality from which he speaks teaches us too much about which we are next to totally ignorant (or unresponsive) that is too essential to our own salvation to worry too much at this stage about his salvation or the salvation of others subject to his "influence."

11

Hopefully not in contradiction to this expressed non-intent, these reflections will include questions to Gutiérrez that reveal areas of his reflection which I cannot at this stage confess as my own theology. Hopefully this will not obscure too much the areas of profound agreement with Gutiérrez and the points where his reflection reveals most strikingly my own unbelief and disobedience to the gospel.

I will include with these questions an indication of the convictions which I share with Gutiérrez. Without claiming in this process to be speaking for the "young evangelical" phenomenon as a whole or for others who have been associated (whether by themselves or others) with this phenomenon, perhaps this combination of "annunciation" and "denunciation" will reveal something of the tension many of us feel between the continuity and discontinuity of our emerging confession with our conservative-evangelical heritage.[6]

I hope especially that this reflection can raise to the surface elements generally associated with the conservative-evangelical tradition to which all of us should be devoting more attention in the interest of a greater obedience to the gospel. This greater attention could be either by way of stronger affirmation or a more consistent negation. Are there, for example, areas of traditionally "evangelical" belief and practice that we should be adopting more boldly, in the interest of greater faithfulness to Christ as well as greater effectiveness in our task of communication to the larger evangelical community? Conversely, are there elements of unbiblical North American cultural consciousness or conservative-evangelical consciousness that still lie dormant in our thought and are still determinative of exegesis and action that we need to isolate, scrutinize, and attempt to eradicate from their place of influence? How can Gutiérrez help us discover these areas? And what is Gutiérrez telling us about the necessity to move courageously forward into the area of a sociopolitical analysis informed by the gospel, to make our obedience to Christ more concrete and our love to our neighbor more effective? Can it be that we are too preoccupied with "what the Bible says" or too comfortable in our enjoyment of the benefits of the consumer society to move radically and courageously forward in such a direction?

With these purposes in view I will proceed in the following manner: I will isolate two large areas of Gutiérrez' thought, selected for their ability to bring into focus what I believe to be some of the central issues his reflection raises for us. The first of these is in the area of hermeneutics and the theological method. The second will focus on salvation, the church, and the world (the kingdom of God). A third area, which would include Marxist and other post-Enlightenment ingredients in Gutiérrez' reflection (including the historicity of existence, an evolutionary philosophy of history, etc.), as well as his analysis of the Latin American situation of dependence, will not be treated separately because of the limits of time and a lack of sufficient competency on the part of the author. Some of these latter matters will surface, of course, in the treatment of the other issues. Hopefully, there will emerge some of the central issues in the third area which have not yet had opportunity to surface. For each of these areas I will try to summarize what I feel to be the main ingredients to Gutiérrez' thinking, points in his position with which I am in substantial agreement, areas in which I have problems with his position, and crucial questions which I think his reflection poses to us.

I should perhaps explain the lack of an exegetical approach to this chapter. I hope that this lack does not rest ultimately in a de facto depreciation of the authority and relevance of the Bible to the issues we are discussing. In my perception, however, the exegetical issues raised are simply too demanding for me to do them justice in the preparation of this essay. Rather than to adopt the convenience of a "proof-texting" method, I would rather leave the exegetical work for a future time. At another level it is important to realize that the issues raised by Gutiérrez will be solved only partly by exegesis and not at all by an exegesis isolated from reflection in directions other than Scripture. Historical, philosophical, and socio-economic issues, constraints, and factors relevant to the prolegomena of exegesis are perhaps the critical issues with which we have to grapple here.

This is not to say that Scripture is irrelevant or even secondary to the task of forming perspectives foundational to the task of exegesis. But it is to raise cautions against the characteristically conservative-evangelical style of going "directly to the Bible" for answers,

13

as though such answers could be found independently of a biblically formed critical reflection on the interpreter's situation, status in obedience, and the inevitable socio-political, philosophical, and cultural constraints on every act of biblical interpretation. In many respects, too great an eagerness to go to Scripture for the "answers" would only reveal to Gutiérrez that at this point of his potentially deepest contribution to us, we have not yet heard him.

A final introductory comment is perhaps in order. The more one ponders *A Theology of Liberation,* the more one realizes that the issues it raises are very complex, leading necessarily into many disciplines of inquiry, historical and contemporary. There is just no way that anyone (and particularly this author at this particular stage in his learning experience) can do anything but "scratch the surface" of these issues or make anything but provisional, incomplete, amateur, and selective probings into the various disciplines of inquiry or facets of contemporary and historical experience that need to be pursued to deal adequately with the issues. In particular, I have had too little opportunity to study Marxist thought to understand or analyze adequately the Marxist components of Gutiérrez' reflection.

In spite of the truth in Gutiérrez' insistence that the critical and all-determining issues (or better, facts) are the division between the oppressor and the oppressed among nations and people and the inevitability of class struggle, I am tempted nevertheless to believe that *A Theology of Liberation* also resurrects classical philosophical and theological issues that have divided the church for centuries. I suspect that these issues, once surfaced, will also divide us in this dialogue into various distinct perspectives, despite a common commitment to social justice integral to our Christian commitment. It would be a fruitful exercise, in fact, to reflect together on just what significance these differences make in actual practice. The relation of faith to reason, the church to the world, faith to history, the Bible to tradition, and the kingdom to the historical process are some of the major ones. Perhaps these are all different ways of looking at a single, core problem, to which might be added its particularly urgent contemporary expressions—the relation of thought to action, theology to social science, and theology to "ideology." And, of course, there is

14

also the issue of the relation between the universal and particular dimensions of salvation, the transcendent and the imminent dimensions of faith and reality, and the divine and human initiative in salvation. I expect all of us live out some personal, intuitive, and provisional "solution" to all of these questions and only infrequently engage in attempts to articulate theoretically our "resolutions" of the dilemmas these questions pose. I expect that this dialogue will be, above all, a conglomerate of "testimonies" as to the different ways these conflicting dimensions come together in our thinking, and, hopefully, the sharing of styles of obedience that these solutions imply.

Hermeneutics and Theological Method: *"Sola Scriptura,"* Ideology, and Historical Praxis

That we begin here should not be interpreted to mean that the central message of *A Theology of Liberation* to us is, in a narrow sense, "methodological." *A Theology of Liberation,* insofar as it is intended for a non-oppressed audience, seems to be intended above all as a profound challenge for Christians in the affluent world to obey the gospel and stop taking refuge in theology as an excuse, a delaying tactic, or, worst of all, an instrument to sanctify the *status quo.*[7] With the help of a Marxist analysis of the causes of injustice and as an essential (or at least the best yet discovered) scientific, historical mediation of Christian obedience, it is a call to radical historical engagement in favor of the oppressed, including a radical denunciation of the oppressive structures of capitalism.[8] Probably most of us here are targets of this challenge in one way or another. Many of us are probably de facto "reformists." The radical evangelicals, insofar as they are unwilling to accept a Marxist analysis as a supplement to the "Strategy of Jesus" or provide a more effective substitute, are probably, from Gutiérrez' perspective, "Biblicists."

At the same time, I expect that even evangelicals of the radical variety will have to take up the challenge of Gutiérrez first of all at the level of philosophical and methodological foundations. One would hope that our consideration of the methodological issue is not undertaken as an escape from the critical importance of the fundamental, larger, ethical challenge. It should be undertaken only in

15

the interest of carving out for ourselves a greater faithfulness to the gospel, a deeper and more profound repentance, and, in the process, a deeper commitment to the struggle for justice. Perhaps it can serve the purpose of presenting another option of radical commitment which, we believe, is more faithful to our understanding of the gospel.

The challenge of Gutiérrez in terms of methodology in theology, I suspect, carries with it deep ramifications for all of us. The central insight at this point seems to be that there is no ideologically neutral theology or exegesis. Grounded, among other places, on the epistemology of Marx and the "sociology of knowledge" of Mannheim, the "theology of liberation" affirms the inevitable socio-economic constraints on all knowledge and human reflection, including theology and exegesis.

If I am understanding Gutiérrez and other advocates of the "theology of liberation" correctly, they are saying more than that knowledge is conditioned by one's experience or historical context. This insight alone presents a great enough challenge, particularly for conservative-evangelicals. But beyond this, the Christian and theologian is also conditioned by an implicit or explicit framework essential to organize his or her experience. This framework influences all knowledge in such a way that it provides a tool by which a person either engages to transform reality, or keep it as it is. Once the Marxist analysis of reality is accepted as the scientific, historical mediation of Christian obedience (i.e., the ideological framework), as it has been by Gutiérrez and others, this central insight is refined further to say that all theological reflection falls on one side or the other of the oppressor-oppressed axis.[9] Virtually all Western or North Atlantic theology, in this analysis, is limited by the historical praxis from which it arises and, whether consciously or not, serves as an instrument to sanctify either reactionary or reformist political options.[10]

Theology is variously defined by Gutiérrez as "the understanding of faith" (*A Theology of Liberation,* p. 3), "critical reflection on praxis" (p. 6), "man's critical reflection of himself, his own basic principles" (p. 11), "reflection on pastoral activity" (p. 11), "critical reflection on Christian praxis in the light of the Word" (p. 13), "critical reflection, the fruit of a confrontation between the Word ac-

16

cepted in faith and historical praxis" (p. 79), and "a critical reflection
—in the light of the Word accepted in faith—on historical praxis and
therefore on the presence of Christians in the world"(p. 145).

I would take the central definition to be "the critical reflection on
historical praxis." But again, I would take this to mean more than
something like "reflection on the situation of the believer in the
world." It is this, but more. Though Gutiérrez uses the term
"praxis" at times in this more general and weaker sense, I sense that
the meaning drifts ultimately towards its more technical sense, consistent with Marx's epistemology.[11] Praxis, therefore, is more than
merely "involvement in a situation," or "practice." It is a particular
kind of involvement informed by a particular kind of analysis within the
historical situation. It is in the last analysis the praxis of participation
in the class struggle to bring about the creation of a new socialist society.
Theology is totally internal to this praxis and deepens one's commitment within it. Transformation of the world, not the discovery or refinement of doctrine as timeless truth, is the goal of theology.[12]

Gutiérrez articulates a theory of revelation consistent with this
emphasis. When we think of his theological methodology in terms of
its underlying theory of revelation, it is possible to detect in his
methodology greater continuity with Roman Catholic tradition than
with the Protestant one, with the higher revelatory value the latter
places on the Bible in relation to ecclesiastical tradition. The fact
that Gutiérrez devotes little concentrated attention to the place of the
Bible in theological reflection and correspondingly more to the wording
and trends in papal encyclicals tends to confirm this analysis.[13]

It should be noted that Miguez-Bonino, by way of contrast, possibly feeling the tensions between a Marxist praxiological approach
and the Protestant *sola Scriptura*, devotes a chapter of his recent
book to the apparent dilemma of conflicting sources of theological
reflection and to how, in the approach of the "theology of liberation,"
the risk of the "ideological captivity" of exegesis can be reduced.[14]

With some continuity, certainly, with the traditional Roman Catholic thought, and with help as well from some distinctive emphases
of contemporary theology ("the church for others," the anthropological trend in theology, etc.) Gutiérrez develops a consistent though

piecemeal view of revelation which gives revelatory character to the historical engagement of the believer in the world and in the historical praxis of the church and only secondarily the Bible or tradition.[15] Correspondingly, the scientific analysis of reality that informs historical praxis becomes all the more determinative in terms of the "substance" of theological reflection. Hermeneutics becomes "political hermeneutics."[16]

Leaving the summary of Gutiérrez' thinking aside, there are several elements of his hermeneutics which, it seems to me, provide needed correctives to traditional evangelical hermeneutics and theological method. Without attempting to be exhaustive, I would identify these (and some of their implications) as the following:

1. Theology (and exegesis) is inevitably influenced by the ideological, cultural, and socio-political values and commitments of the interpreter/theologian. Standard evangelical textbooks on hermeneutics have been next to silent on this critical dimension of interpretation. The emergence of the "theology of liberation" and other distinctive theological and interpretative approaches from the Third World as well as from women, Blacks, and other oppressed groups in the U.S. forces, it seems to me, something approaching a major adjustment in standard hermeneutical approaches. It exposes the myth of objective exegesis and the tendency to equate any fruit of exegesis or any theological construction with revelation itself. For evangelicals, who have traditionally found in the doctrine of inerrancy a final refuge against theological relativism, this new development would appear to have significant implications and could signal the beginning of a new phase in the discussion on Scripture.[17]

2. Theological reflection, for the sake of minimizing unconscious cultural captivity and assisting faithful and effective proclamation of the gospel, has to become a *"multi-directional reflection."*[18] The "ideology criticism" to which José Miguez-Bonino calls us is a crucial priority, especially for those of us who have tended to view our theological reflection as something done in isolation from our commitment to American values and institutions.[19] All attempts to analyze movements like the "theology of liberation"

18

on the basis of exegesis not coupled with a critical self-analysis of the interpreter's attachment to structures which oppress the poor will rightly be suspect. Theology, in this construction, should include reflection on the historical and contemporary functioning of the believer and the church in relation to society. Accordingly, it should help refine elements of "mind-set" and practice incompatible with the gospel. It should include reflection on Scripture as the norm for a "sanctified" consciousness and practice.[20] It should include a socio-political analysis of the larger society and world-historical reality of which the believer and the church are inevitably a part. The purpose of this latter reflection will be to determine expressions of disbelief and disobedience in secular consciousness and structures as a basis for prophetic/evangelistic, personal and structural proclamation ("denunciation"/"annunciation"). It should also develop an awareness of the interconnections between structures and the injustices they perpetuate and thereby develop a base for an effective call to change as the fruit of repentance. This, in turn, should enable greater concreteness in our expression of love to the poor. All this implies a new working partnership between theology and the social sciences necessary to carry this multi-direction analysis forward.

3. All theology arises from a situation of radical immersion in the world and in the historical process—a situation of integrated spiritual-historical-social conflict. The theologian, whether a "professional" or a simple believer, engages in theological reflection (including exegesis) in the midst of a struggle between the forces of darkness and light, amidst the not yet completed battle with the "principalities and powers." As H. Berkhof and others have pointed out, Christ's ongoing battle with the powers is not merely a "spiritual" one, but shows itself in the conflict on the level of social and political institutions and cultural traditions.[21] The theologian-believer cannot undertake his or her reflection as though he or she were above the battle and not engaged in it (and, possibly, even on the wrong side!).

4. The "truth" of theology or its correspondence to revelation has

to be verified partially in terms of its expression in practice. It seems to me that the essential insight of Gutiérrez regarding the complementary nature of orthodoxy and orthopraxis is a correct and biblical one.

5. For Gutiérrez, theology as reflection on praxis is an integral part of the transforming of man and society which is the essence of praxis.[22] Theology is an instrument and servant of this process. Gutiérrez gives expression to an important biblical insight here which reveals a fatal weakness in traditional theological reflection, whether "evangelical" or "liberal." In my thinking, theology should be radically transforming reflection—transforming of the believer-theologian into conformity to the image of Christ (the "new man" in Pauline terminology) and the church into the new humanity constituted in Christ's resurrection. It also should constitute a transformation of the world, insofar as this as an aspect of prophetic evangelism as a call to radical obedience to Christ and into the humanity of the church. Gutiérrez is right in his assertion that such transformation cannot be only "spiritual" or "internal." The transformation that takes place through theological reflection should include the transformation of consciousness *vis a vis* false values inherited from the world and a radical transformation of relationships with structures that oppress the poor. A radically new obedience should be the end goal and actual result of all theology.

But it is clear that while accepting various "core insights" of Gutiérrez I have departed significantly from him in their outworking. Here I will enter into critical dialogue in the interest of clarifying where the critical differences lie. As I have studied *A Theology of Liberation* and compared it with my own perspective, I have concluded that at the most basic level the differences lie in the different value he and I place on the Bible in comparison to other elements of the theological reflection process (i.e., ecclesiastical tradition and practice and the socio-political analysis of our situation). This difference is perhaps rooted in my inability to ascribe revelational value —or better, what traditional Reformed systematic theology called "special" revelational value—to these other elements.

Perhaps at an even more basic level there is involved here a different way of lining up reason—"political reason" in Gutiérrez' case —and revelation.[23] I expect that in this instance Gutiérrez and I represent historically different ways of resolving the "Christ and culture" problem. H. Richard Niebuhr describes the typical difference between the "Christ against culture" and the "Christ of culture" models.[24] Gutiérrez' position stretches the limits of Niebuhr's typology in several respects. His dynamic view of history seems to place him outside any of the standard types Niebuhr isolates. As a result, his position seems to be a dialectical synthesis between "Christ against (capitalist-oppressor) culture," "Christ of (socialist-oppressed) culture," and possibly even "Christ transforming culture" (the process of liberation).

Any dependence on Niebuhr's typology in this context has to be accompanied by a full appreciation of the fact that the central claim the "theology of liberation" makes with respect to North Atlantic theology is that it represents a fatal accommodation to the culture of liberal democracy and capitalism. I expect that in the long run Gutiérrez and I are agreed about that. I would hope eventually, if not now, to succeed in outlining an approach which will present the potential of a radically biblical critique of Western culture—including capitalism— without at the same time coming down where Gutiérrez does, either in the direction of a reduced biblical message or the adoption of a Marxist strategy for change.

It seems to me, however, that in the use which Gutiérrez makes of the Bible, and particularly in the way he resolves the revelation and reason problem, his position falls into the "accommodationist" approach. By contrast, mine is probably still operating somewhere within the "biblicist" framework, social justice concerns notwithstanding.[25] I expect that the difference is the most fundamental one between us and explains ultimately all the other differences that follow.

It seems to me that the Bible has ended up doing too little for Gutiérrez at several levels:

1. His theology or philosophy of history has come too little from biblical eschatology and too much from Marxism and other contemporary sources. The use of the O.T. imagery of the Exodus

seems to be revealing here. There is certainly the aspect of biblical revelation that is most susceptible to the evolutionary (though dialectical) view of history that seems to underlie Gutiérrez' thinking. But as I go to the N.T., where Christ is the fulfillment of the Exodus, I see less of this kind of a model with its optimistic language of bringing into being a qualitatively new society in this particular stage of redemptive history, either within or without the church. At this point I think I am closer to the "interim" approach of Reinhold Niebuhr. It seems to me that he was both biblical and "scientific" in saying that all historical achievements will be tainted with evil short of God's fulfillment of history.[26] Accordingly, to talk as freely and optimistically about a new man and new society as Gutiérrez does or to put as much hope in the new socialist state as he does seems to be something less than sufficiently biblical. "A "canon within a canon" seems to have been selected here out of a valid concern to make the gospel relevant to the aspirations of the oppressed for liberation and concretize God's (and the church's) identification with the poor. But as with all such selections, not enough of the whole Bible comes through or is allowed to challenge our thinking and perspective at enough points.[27]

2. Further, the Bible seems to function too little as a controlling influence in the "scientific" analysis of reality which Gutiérrez feels is essential as a historical mediation of Christian obedience. I expect that at this point we are at the core of the classical faith (revelation) and reason problem. But the critical question for me is this: admitting that the Bible does not give us all we need to insure a faithful obedience to Christ in the midst of the struggle for justice, does it function at all in forming the consciousness which we take to the task of social analysis? Does it give any clues as to what to look for in our search for root causes of poverty and injustice? What is the function and potential of the Bible to transform the very perspective we learn on the level of sociopolitical analysis? Admitting the importance of the supplementation or even the integration of theological and social scientific reflection on reality, how in this integration does the Bible op-

22

erate as canon and norm? This is perhaps the critical question which none of us have sufficiently answered. Gutiérrez is certainly correct in saying that one's Christian commitment gives the Christian social scientist a bias against oppression and even against the sanctity and necessity of the world order. But on the other hand, how can the Bible function not only at the level of creating an *a priori* bias against the current structures, but also sufficiently as a check against new idolatries that creep in at the point of our projections for something new?[28]

3. From my perspective, the Bible functions too minimally for Gutiérrez also on the level of discovering how the Christian should respond to whatever data his or her analysis of reality uncovers about the existence of class struggle, etc. I am in a curious tension here between those who deny (or are oblivious to) the existence of class struggle and those who want to join it wholeheartedly on the "right side." I have not studied Marxism, capitalism, or just plain reality enough to know the extent to which the class struggle hypothesis holds up under "biased-for the poor" scrutiny. It seems to me that those who *have,* inevitably work (struggle?) to keep what they have and, unconsciously, have what they have mostly at others' expense. But, again, Gutiérrez seems to have so elevated the realm of biblical revelation from the realm of political reason (or so radically fused them) that the Bible comes up with too little for him in terms of how I, as a Christian, respond to these facts. As Miguez-Bonino summarizes Gutiérrez:

> This assumption of Marxism—which is not tantamount to an uncritical acceptance of all its philosophy—is decisive for the theological task and indicates, as Giulio Girardi has said, a 'qualitative leap' from the humanist or spiritualist inspiration of 'social concern' to an engagement mediated through a scientific (Marxist) analysis. How is this mediation established? It is quite evident that one cannot expect to extract from the Bible models of political or economic organization applicable to society. Gutiérrez solves the problem by distinguishing two levels: that of political action, which is eminently rational/scientific, and that of faith, which is the libera-

tion from sin and the access to fellowship with God and with all men.[29]

In contrast to Gutiérrez here, I want to separate the rational and scientific level less totally from that of faith and revelation and, accordingly, want to find in the Bible more (and in scientific analysis less) in terms of the process and mechanisms through which God is in fact liberating man, the proper styles of my participation in the liberation process, and even models of economic and political organization through which this liberation comes to fruition. Admittedly, another difference with Gutiérrez interjects at this point—i.e., the different ways we understand the relationship between the church and the world. I look for the liberation to be happening predominantly (though not exclusively) within the new humanity of the church, and the models found in the Bible more directly applicable here than in the society-at-large. But again, this different perspective on the church and the world rests ultimately on the different uses we make of the Bible and the contrasting levels of detail relevant to the present which we expect to find there.

In my pilgrimage from fundamentalism I am looking for an approach to social justice concerns that does justice to the "biblical realist" instincts of my upbringing. At this point I am finding something close to the right kind of synthesis in the Anabaptist tradition. John Howard Yoder's *The Politics of Jesus* develops some of the foundations, it seems to me, for an approach which enables the church to speak prophetically within a capitalist society (and even attempting to change the society through the instrument of a prophetic evangelism) while maintaining the essential content of a N.T. eschatology.[30] This approach also allows the Bible to fill in some of the main ingredients of the content of Christian obedience. *A Theology of Liberation,* by contrast, seems to find too little in the Bible, and too much in a Marxist analysis, all the way down to the style and methods of participation in the liberation process. As a result, the Bible seems to function too much as merely a book of illustrations for a story written essentially from other sources or as an explication of the "hidden" ground and meaning of a process that could well move forward with it.

24

From this general approach to the Bible several other problems arise for Gutiérrez' position, it seems to me. How, for example, does one decide (when doing theology at the level of *A Theology of Liberation*) which church's praxis one should reflect on? Admitting the ideological conditioning of all theology, can the Bible break through to tell us which ideology is better, yours or mine? Otherwise, aren't we left with a position that says your theology isn't wrong and mine right, they are just different? Haven't we simply transferred the verification question from biblical interpretation and theology to a "scientific" analysis of reality? Doesn't the burden of convincing the capitalist that he is wrong rest too heavily then on the unlikely possibility of getting him to accept the correctness of a Marxist social analysis (which by its own admission is not arrived at from a neutral stance)?

These questions are very pertinent to the matter of how people are going to be convinced of the evils of the existing system. Somehow I have more trust in the Bible and the Holy Spirit at this point than I do in social analysis of which the Bible is something like a mirror image. To be sure, a lot of facts, data, and even theoretical perspectives from Marx are necessary to supplement the Bible in this consciousness-raising process. But for me the Bible would be the most important element. And apart from the working of the Holy Spirit accompanying the Bible in such a process of discipling and evangelizing, I really have little hope at all in convincing my evangelical friends about that truth that there is in what Marx has to say.

But having said all of this, Gutiérrez still leaves us, it seems to me, with a lot of challenges we have yet fully to meet. I would like to put these to my partners in this dialogue, and especially to my "radical evangelical" colleagues.

1. Have we moved far enough towards finding the social-analytical instruments (our equivalent of what Marx seems to provide Gutiérrez) with which to supplement our appeal to the "strategy of Jesus" and our frequent (and probably ineffective) calls to "repentance"? Are we expecting to find too much in the Bible by way of a strategy for change that leads us to depreciate the need for socio-political analysis?

25

2. How can we demonstrate more in practice that our non-Marxist approach is not at the same time a concession to reformism or does not rest ultimately in a captivity to the ideology of capitalism and liberal democracy?
3. In our appeals to Scripture are we too oblivious to the plurality of models and theologies within the Bible? Are we also adopting a "canon within a canon" approach and finding in the N.T. only those concepts which seem to correspond with the model of evangelism and community-building to which we are committed?[31]
4. Do we do sufficient justice in our hermeneutic to the distance that separates us from the political and cultural situation of the N.T.? Does the movement of the historical and cultural formation process since the N.T. nullify our attempts to find so much of relevance to a strategy of change in the N.T.? Does our hermeneutic do sufficient justice to the hermeneutical implications of the "delay" of the parousia?[32]

The Kingdom of God: Salvation, the Church, and the Historical Struggle for Liberation

Under this main heading I will consider an integrated complex of issues related to salvation and the kingdom of God. This will include Gutiérrez' view of salvation, the kingdom, and the church as they relate to the historical struggle of liberation.

If I understand Gutiérrez correctly, he has for all practical purposes equated the biblical notion of salvation and the oppressed's struggle for justice. To be sure, he believes that the gospel adds deepening perspective to the meaning of liberation. He speaks in clear terms about sin as the root cause of oppression.[33] He also insists that the liberation that Christ offers is the deepest level of the meaning of liberation and that the other two levels (aspirations of the oppressed and the historical process/struggle of liberation) are incomplete without it.[34] But it is clear that the way salvation is accomplished is in the liberation process understood as engagement in the class struggle for its eventual overcoming in the classless society:

To work, to transform this world, is to become a man and to build the human community; it is also to save. Likewise, to struggle against misery and exploitation and to build a just society is already to be part of the saving action, which is moving towards its complete fulfillment. All this means that building the temporal city is not simply a stage of 'humanization' or 'pre-evangelization' as was held in theology up until a few years ago.[35]

Of a piece with this emphasis is Gutiérrez' rejection of the "quantitative" notion of salvation. In this view the mission of the church was conceived of as saving numbers of souls. The church was viewed as the center of God's saving activity.[36] Gutiérrez' thinking here corresponds to his radical integration of salvation history and liberation-struggle history. The kingdom of God is identical to the struggle of liberation as far as its mechanism of fulfillment is concerned. It is distinct from the process insofar as the complete fulfillment of the kingdom is always future and always reveals present achievements as provisional, impermanent, and incomplete.[37] Correspondingly, evangelization and conversion take on a radically different meaning. Evangelization is to announce the presence of the love of God in the "historical becoming of mankind."[38] Conversion is conversion to our neighbor and the oppressed person manifested by engagement in the struggle for his/her liberation.[39]

As I reflect on Gutiérrez' view and his rejection of the church's previous understandings, it is obvious to me that he and I are in many respects on the same pilgrimage. He is absolutely right in denouncing as unbiblical the church's individualization and spiritualization of salvation and its privatization of sin. It is certainly true that there is no conversion to God without a conversion to neighbor and no biblical evangelization that does not have as its end goal the call to participate in the struggles of the poor. But despite this great continuity of concern, at some point our paths again have diverged.

Part of the reason for this divergence (and perhaps even its root cause) is the universalism of Gutiérrez' soteriology. I expect that a merging of the kingdom and history (and the church and the world) and an understanding of salvation as humanization was arrived at from this root theological commitment even before Gutiérrez came to hold that a Marxian perspective is essential for true humanization.

Further, it seems that in his valid rejection of the "verticalist" and "spiritualist" heresy in the church's understanding of sin, salvation, and evangelization, Gutiérrez' solution is in danger of moving too far in the opposite direction. Recognizing the critical importance of what José Miguez-Bonino has to say about the depreciation of human work in traditional Christian understandings, it seems to me that Gutiérrez has not done sufficient justice to the Pauline doctrine of justification and its place in a total biblical view of salvation.[40]

The Protestant view and hermeneutic may be overbalanced in the direction of a preoccupation with justification. But I would like to have seen more treatment of this theme in *A Theology of Liberation* than I found. Apart from this absence of treatment, the view of salvation that is presented seems to do insufficient justice to the fact that salvation is in the end God's work, not man's.[41] Perhaps greater use of the Pauline notion of "works of faith" (i.e., works after faith) and its contrast to "works of the law" (works before faith) could provide a view of salvation which does not diminish the critical necessity of engagement in the struggle for justice while maintaining the element of grace and the priority of divine initiative.

The emphasis of Gutiérrez on salvation and liberation as a human work also brings us into the orbit of a couple of other critical issues— the priority of proclamation in liberation and the centrality of the cross as the paradigm for Christian involvement in social change. For Paul the priority placed on the proclamation of the gospel was of a single piece with his conviction that salvation came by faith apart from the works of the law.[42] Proclamation was the medium of communication appropriate to this insight. It was the vehicle by which people would be led to an awareness that the demands of God's righteousness had been met for them in Jesus Christ. Faith as (among other things) the acceptance of the truth of this fact was the appropriate response.

Achievement of liberation from sin through the gift of the Holy Spirit and incorporation into Christ (and His body) was received at the point of this initial faith. The outworking of this "spiritual" liberation into its various historical and creation-oriented directions follows in temporal sequence, it seems to me, in the life of the community of faith and its action in the world. This is not to "spiritualize" salvation. Salvation includes the total scope of the new life—the new creation—received in real (though incomplete) form through the working of the Spirit and the exercise of love in the community, and totally at the consummation of history with the return of Christ.

Proclamation, then, should be at the center of a biblical strategy of social change.[43] The medium itself emphasizes that the work of liberation is God's and not man's. But the response of authentic faith always produces in its wake the works of faith. These works express in concrete reality the restoration of human work to its original vocation as service to God. This also becomes the instrument for the further unfolding of Christ's ongoing program of liberation of man and creation.

Consideration of this issue of the divine and human initiative in liberation brings us also to the matter of the Christian's position in the class struggle and the resort to counterviolence. To be sure, the creation is caught in a struggle of power in which the rich secure and protect their wealth through institutionalized violence which can be "effectively" challenged only by counterviolence. The class struggle in this sense is a historical fact. But the critical question is how the Christian relates to this larger reality and how, in the midst of this struggle, God is achieving our liberation.

If a new society short of the consummation is established as a goal and totally human and worldly means are seen as the only instruments with which to achieve it, then something like the Marxist strategy for change is the only option. But it seems that we have to rest with the fact that for one reason or another God is not achieving liberation in that way. Why else would Christ have died on the cross and rejected the "Zealot option"? To be sure, God is bringing about the liberation of creation and the liberation of man—the complete, spiritual, social, and political liberation. But He seems to be doing it over time and through the means of proclamation and calling into being a distinct, liberated servant community in the midst of the world. Even the true church is not totally liberated. The new humanity is a heavenly reality whose earthly achievements always fall

29

short of the prototype. But authentic liberation is taking place in the true church nevertheless.

The strategy of the cross is a complement to the priority of proclamation. It is a witness to the fact that mini-liberations in contemporary history begin with the radical transformation accomplished by God the Holy Spirit at the point of faith and continued within the community of faith. It is witness as well to the fact that the final liberation and the creation of the qualitatively new world order takes place at the end of history with the intervention of God in judgment on the side of the poor and the faithful.

All this is significant, it seems to me, at the point of strategy. The Christian community should be a part of the class struggle first of all by being one with the poor in being a victim of the struggle. A church that is not the victim of the class struggle has nothing credible to say about the issue of violence. Not to be a victim of the struggle is to be a perpetrator of the struggle. To sanctify "non-violence" while silently condoning its institutionalized forms is hypocrisy. But given the stance of victim of the struggle, the community's persistence in the strategy of the cross and the priority of proclamation is essential to maintain its witness in the initiative of God in liberation and the utter urgency of the response of faith for forgiveness of sins against the poor. Is not counterviolence prior to faith "works of the law"? Doesn't counterviolence after faith fail to depend on the power of the Spirit or to carry on in Christ's absence His strategy of the cross? Isn't it to take upon oneself the act of final judgment that belongs to Christ alone?

Gutiérrez' view of salvation seems to react too far against the notion that salvation is more than reconciliation to one's neighbor. There is a brokenness between God and man rooted in man's rebellion from God that needs to be healed. To be sure, traditional Protestant theology (and conservative-evangelical theology) have overemphasized this aspect to the detriment of the horizontal dimension of reconciliation. Justification by faith has been abstracted from other Pauline themes in too one-sided a fashion and the "forensic" aspect of justification emphasized at the expense of other espects. But the correction against this heresy is best made, it seems to me, not by

30

something approaching total rejection, but by restoring more of the original balance.[44]

Whereas the matter of hermeneutics and theological method may have served to point out the basic foundational difference between Gutiérrez and what I perceive to be something approaching a common perspective of evangelical social activists, the issue of salvation and evangelization may pull to the surface what I see as the major contrast at the point of tactics and strategy. Whereas Gutiérrez seems to reject the quantitative model of salvation and evangelization altogether by means of a radical inversion of the task of evangelization into the struggle for liberation, evangelical social activists (or, at least, the "radical" type) are struggling for what I would call a radicalization of the quantitative model.

Evangelical social activists do not want to concede that the basic structure or model of evangelism as disciple-making and church planting was wrong. The trouble with the old model was not the model itself, but the individualistic and spiritualistic notion of sin and salvation that accompanied it. This meant a tendency to privatize sin, to emphasize the horizontal at the expense of the vertical, and resulted in "disciples" all too naive about the injustices of the present social order and too comfortable within the womb of the consumer society. The old model, in this perspective, does not need to be disposed of or exchanged for a Marxist strategy of change. It needs rather to be radicalized and biblicized and even politicized.

There may be an authentic conversion to one's neighbor—i.e., commitment to the process of liberation—without it being at the same time true conversion to God. But open profession of Christ's name is essential if one is to receive full liberation or even to be an effective participant in the full liberation of others. At the same time, there can be no true conversion to God which is not at the same time a commitment to radical engagement in the struggles of the poor.[45]

Evangelization, then, is the process of proclaiming the past and present liberating work of Christ in such a way that people are led into the ongoing process of this twofold conversion and into communities of faith demonstrating and proclaiming the lordship of Christ. As such, these communities will be incarnating in their life-

31

style the transformation of values that accompany salvation, demonstrating the contrast between these values and the values underlying the oppressive structures of the larger society, and engaging in prophetic/evangelistic action and proclamation to individuals and structures in the world.

It is clear that one of the major points of contrast between this perspective and that of Fr. Gutiérrez is at the level of ecclesiology.[46] In this view the church is more than the sacrament of a world-historical process. Without necessarily claiming to be the exclusive context in which salvation and liberation takes place, the church—to the extent that it is the true church—is the community where liberation in its various dimensions is most authentically, though imperfectly, achieved. This perspective shares the alienation which Gutiérrez feels with the institutional church. It operates on the assumption—perhaps without clearly articulating it—that the true church is something closer to a minority that is radically and prophetically engaged within the larger community. But in contrast to Gutiérrez' tendency to break down the church/world distinction and to reduce the contribution of the church to the liberation process to a sacramental, "mystery revealing" function, this perspective claims that the deepest dimensions of liberation happen not in the secular-historical struggle, but in the struggle of the Christ-confessing community within this larger historical struggle. In this view the true church becomes something like the part of the larger Christian community committed to justice plus the part of the justice struggle openly professing allegiance to Jesus Christ. The task of the church is not to play down its identity within the struggle, but to unashamedly invite people to find their aspirations for justice fulfilled in Christ and realized in the Christian community.

Admittedly, this perspective comes into the lineup of liberation options with a tremendous disadvantage. The historical identification of the church with the rich and the powerful makes the message close to incredible. As a result the perspective requires a prophetic proclamation to (or even a disengagement from) the established church—including the evangelical one. And it requires that a premium be placed on the demonstration in small, minority Christian communities that what is said in the message to the world—that true multi-dimension liberation happens in the true church—is true and verifiable by social-scientific analysis.

The vigor with which this option has been contrasted with Gutiérrez', however, should not blind us to the unmet challenges that his insights still leave with us. I would isolate some of these challenges as follows:

1. Does our "disciple-making," church-centered view do full justice to the work of God in and through liberation movements that take place outside the church? Do we need a more historically dynamic update of the old doctrines of providence, general revelation, or common grace through which we can affirm that struggles for justice display something of the saving work of God in history? Is the saving work of Christ in history accomplished only in the wake of the evangelizing work of the disciple-makers and only in radical Christian communities?

2. Is there in our praxis an aloofness from the demanding task of social analysis that amounts to a de facto spiritualizing and privatizing of sin and salvation? Does our preoccupation with "faithfulness" and our fear of compromise in the pursuit of "effectiveness" incorporate too little of Gutiérrez' concern that love be concrete and historically effective?

3. Does our emphasis on community-building and our rejection of reformist political action on the one hand or Marxist engagement on the other run the risk of being understood as an introversion of concern and by the same amount fail to demonstrate sufficiently the other-directedness of the love of Christ?

4. How do we answer the traditional ecclesiological problem of the "marks of the church"? Are we trying to claim continuity with the evangelical church and tradition on the one hand while feeling at a deeper level that the vast majority of this church and tradition has not and does not display the true marks of the church? (How can we "have our [evangelical] cake and eat it too"?) Or, on the other hand, do the differences among us—like the division between radical and reformist approaches to change—reveal a tendency in practice (we would probably never admit it in theory)

to elevate tactical considerations to the level of a "mark" of the church?[47] How do we explain theologically our greater "spiritual" unity with the non-Christian radical than with the "Christian" conservative or reactionary?

5. Does our disciple-making approach (or the way we carry it out in practice) lean too heavily on the notion that society can be changed by changing individuals, or that authentic conversions can take place without an antecedent change in political and social structures?[48] Are our appeals to "conversion" and "repentance" too individualistic? Do they recognize too little the unlikelihood of radical transformation prior to the formation of a social and community context supportive of such transformations?

6. Finally, do we talk too glibly and naively about "model communities"? Where have they happened in history? Where are they now? Are we sufficiently aware how totally submerged any community is within the larger culture and that "transformation" in relation to the larger culture normally has been less, in retrospect, than such model communities thought they were achieving at the time?

Notes

1. "Perhaps the positive aspect of the enormous repercussion of our Christian babbling in Latin America is this very point: the testimonial offered by the commitment to a decided struggle against capitalistic oppression. If this is what has awakened a certain interest, it is good. It states clearly: Don't take our writings for something which they are not; don't transform us into a consumer product to make up for your impotence; don't be spectators of our small achievements, nor project on Latin America an image of compensations; and finally, all of you, each in his own context, enter into the same struggle. . . ." Hugo Assmann, "Basic Aspects of Theological Reflection in Latin America: A critical evaluation of the 'Theology of Liberation.'" *Risk* 9, 2 (1973), 28.

2. *Ibid.,* 11.

3. "Maybe it is easier for us in Latin America to perceive the contradictions because of our historical context. Okay, it is easier for us to begin our Easter, but I cannot accept that you are not able to do the same. The

question really is whether you are interested in doing it in your place."
Paulo Freire, *Risk, op. cit.,* 65.
4. A Marxist style analysis of this whole process of reflection and dialogue
we are perpetually involved in is not difficult to visualize. Could it be that
the leisure and status we enjoy in being here is evidence in itself that we
have little intention to go beyond the 'pre-theology' of which Assmann
warns us and into a radical commitment to the gospel and justice? (See
Assman, *Risk, op. cit.,* 26.)
5. "Another thing that I have perceived on different occasions in Europe is
that when we are explaining our position the Europeans are really curious
to understand what we are trying to do, what we are trying to say. But
there is a background of ideology which means that behind much curiosity
there is a certain paternalistic attitude. For example, many Europeans
listen to us in the same style in which some parents—not good parents—
listen to their children. *'Oh yes, let's listen to what little John can tell us.'*
It is not conscious, it is because of your historical experience: you have
commanded the world, you have imposed on Africa, Latin America and
Asia your way of thinking, your technology, your values, your civilization,
your goods, your humanism . . . and so on." Freire, *op. cit.,* 58.
6. I do not intend to assume by the employment of these adjectives ("evangelical," "young evangelical") that the terms are unambiguous in their
denotation. Nor do I intend to pass judgment on the faith of those not
included in particular "evangelical" structures. By "evangelical" or "conservative-evangelical" I would understand that segment of Protestantism
arising either from the Reformed and Lutheran Reformation or from the
revival movements of the 18th century which in the midst of the funda-
mentalist-modernist controversy came also to adopt doctrinal positions and
(especially a view of Scripture) formulated to withstand the threat of
"higher criticism." The stance of these people and groups with respect to
the ecumenical movement I would regard as a factor of secondary importance. The extension of Barth's influence and his critique of the liberalism among many of the "conciliar churches" complicates the picture
somewhat, as does the existence of the "Biblical realist" Anabaptist and
Mennonite movement.

The fact that some of the people we would now regard as "evangelicals"
were minimally influenced by revivalism and maximally preoccupied with
the fight against higher criticism or vice versa is revealed in the diversity
within evangelicalism illustrated by the presence in the larger phenomenon
of both Wesleyan Methodists and Orthodox Presbyterians and Missouri
Synod Lutherans. Don Dayton, if I understand his recent series in *The
Post American* correctly, has been highlighting for us the radical social
engagement (now largely dissipated) of the Wesleyan component of "evangelicalism," calling the group to its roots distinctive from other "evan-

gelicals" in the process. I expect that there is a third major component of evangelicalism, namely, the dispensationalist one, which is more coterminous with "fundamentalism" in the narrower sense and is fairly distinct from either the Wesleyan or Calvinist-Lutheran sectors, both in terms of formative historical influences and contemporary mind-set. Analyses of "evangelical social concern" probably fail for the most part to be discriminating enough of the different components within evangelicalism and the historical influences which have formed them. By the same measure they may be guilty of caricature and correspondingly less effective in leading people in these groups toward a social commitment that draws on distinctive components in their tradition. Don Dayton's series is an exception to this and, hopefully, the beginning of a new trend towards more discriminating analysis.

7. See, for example, Rubem Alves, "Christian Realism, Ideology of the Establishment," *Christianity and Crisis,* Sept. 17, 1973, 173-176.

8. There seems to be a difference among liberation theologians as to the extent and intensity of their commitment to a distinctively Marxist social analysis. Assmann, for example, seems more unbendingly Marxist than does Gutiérrez. Miguez talks more cautiously than either Gutiérrez or Assmann about the acceptability of a Marxist perspective within a Christian framework, perhaps because of the instincts his Protestant tradition gives him about *sola Scriptura* in hermeneutics. (See his *Doing Theology in a Revolutionary Situation* [Philadelphia: Fortress, 1975], especially pp. 96-98.) The evangelical Orlando Costas speaks of the distinctive character of the theology of liberation *vis a vis* social analysis on an even less particular and potentially "threatening" level (i.e., to other evangelicals and to the *sola Scriptura* principle) by speaking merely of a "structuralist" vs. a "functionalist" sociological approach. (*The Church and Its Mission* [Wheaton: Tyndale House, 1974], pp. 225-227.)

9. The term "ideology" is used with identical ethical overtones (i.e., negative) by both Marxists and non-Marxists in describing what each perceives to be the erroneous mind-set *vis a vis* the static or transformable character of reality on the part of the other. I would take the classical Marxist usage to be that captured in Mannheim's distinction between "utopia" as the intra-historical and history-transforming projections of the oppressed and "ideology" as the equivalent mental operations of the oppressor, undertaken in their case for the maintenance of the established order (see Gutiérrez, *TL,* pp. 234-235, and note 120, p. 240). Gutiérrez sticks quite closely to this classical usage, limiting the term largely to its negative sense. Miguez-Bonino, on the other hand, uses the term in an ethically neutral sense to cover the analysis of the structure of reality by both the oppressor and the oppressed (*op. cit.,* pp. 94-95). Non-Marxists traditionally use the term only in a negative sense for what they regard as the

imposition on "neutral," scientific observation of Marxist dogma or, if the non-Marxists are Christian critics of Marxist Christians, the imposition of Marxist categories on biblical revelation. Here I have adopted Miguez' usage.

10. "All we have today in Latin America are reactionary, reformist, or revolutionary readings of what we have called 'germinal events of the Christian faith.' Significant and fruitful self-criticism or dialogue can only take place when we consciously assume our own praxis and reflect from within it— or are converted to one another." Miguez-Bonino, *op. cit.*, p. 99.

11. Perhaps the best single quote here is in *Theology of Liberation*, p. 11. See also Gutiérrez' emphasis on praxis as "concrete and creative service to others" (pp. 10, 11) coupled with the emphasis on the necessity of true charity to express itself by engagement in the class struggle (p. 275). See also note 31, p. 18, p. 49, and his isolation of Marxist epistemology as one of the factors contributing to the praxiological approach in theology (pp. 9, 10).

12. *Ibid.*, p. 10.

13. References to the use of the Bible in Gutiérrez can be found in the following places: pp. 12, 14, 35, 37, 134, 152. The notion of the "Word of God" occurs many times, but I suspect that this is not a precisely equivalent term for the Bible. The most explicit quote on the relation of "revelation," tradition, and contemporary experience in theological reflection is on p. 12.

14. Miguez-Bonino, *op. cit.,* pp. 96-102.

15. Gutiérrez arrives from various directions to the position that the church, history, and the act of love to the neighbor in history are sources of revelation. The Word of God is incarnate in the community (8); the Spirit is present in the church (11); the "church for others" idea serves as a bridge from the church to the historical struggle of humanization as a *"locus theologicus"* (8, 12 see also 79); encounter with God is in concrete actions towards others (195; "Christ in the neighbor," pp. 196ff.); the church and all of history is the temple of God (194, 201); God is revealed in the doing of justice (238); and man is the "sacrament" (revealer) of God (295).

16. Gutiérrez, *op. cit.,* p. 13; note 45, p. 19.

17. One wonders if the view of science which assumed the objectivity of the scientist, placed the burden in evangelical hermeneutics on the factual reliability of the *text,* and elevated the inerrancy discussion to the top of the evangelical agenda has not now revealed itself as outdated, or, at least, beside the point of the contemporary discussion. This may signal a shift in focus in the discussion among evangelicals on Scripture from statements we affirm about the text to how Scripture functions in actual experience, especially in the transformation of the interpreter. Will it also signal a shift from a dependence on Scripture as the sole defense against

relativism and heresy, towards a placing of greater emphasis on the work of the Holy Spirit and the corrective influence on interpretation of a multi-cultural Christian community? Could the charismatic movement with its emphasis on the former and Anabaptism with its emphasis on the latter contribute to the development of an evangelical approach to hermeneutics able to find and keep its bearings in the face of this new challenge? The beginning of discussion on these issues was perhaps foreshadowed in René Padilla's address at Lausanne ("Evangelism and the World," *Let the Earth Hear His Voice* [Minneapolis: World Wide Publications, 1975], pp. 116-146) as well as in the debate surrounding the use of Scripture in (and around) the evangelical feminists' movement.

18. "Theology" here does not imply something done by the professional. I agree with Gutiérrez that everyone has a theology in rough outline and does theology at some level of sophistication.

19. *Op. cit.,* pp. 91, 95.

20. I would distinguish "theology" (as all reflection, whether sophisticated and self-conscious or not, on the meaning of the Christian faith in the midst of the world) from "exegesis" (discovering the meaning of particular biblical texts through historical and grammatical analysis) and "biblical theology" (the "scientific" process of reconstructing what the biblical authors said in a way that does justice to the internal structure of their thought). The latter two tasks are essential ingredients in the theological process but are no less subject to cultural influences than the parts of theological reflection that go in "extra-biblical" directions. The importance of exegesis for "liberating the text for a new obedience" is pointed out by Miguez, *op. cit.,* p. 102.

21. H. Berkhof, *Christ and the Powers* (Scottdale: Herald Press, 1962).

22. The thinking of Gutiérrez on the "New Society" is found in the following places: pp. 26-27, 28, 29, 30, 31, 32, 37, 48, 88, 91, 111, 135, 157. The concept of the "New Man" appears on pp. 32, 33, 91, 111, 145, 146.

23. Gutiérrez himself places his position within the context of the faith and reason problem as follows: he finds continuity between his position and Thomas Aquinas' view of theology as rational knowledge, i.e., a meeting of faith and reason and especially (now) reason as informed by the social sciences (p. 5); the "reason" which faith meets in theology has become "political reason" (p. 47). Miguez describes Gutiérrez' solution to the faith/reason problem as "distinguishing two levels: that of political action, which is eminently rational/scientific, and that of faith, which is the liberation from sin and the access to fellowship with God and with all men" (*op. cit.,* p. 71); Miguez himself operates on a similar basis, speaking of the realm of human rationality as distinct from the level of faith, and a "realm where God has invited man to be *on his own*" (p. 98; see also pp. 103-104). Hence Miguez repeatedly speaks of the class struggle hy-

pothesis as entirely within the realm of empirical investigation.

This, of course, may be true. But doesn't the Marxist analysis as adopted by Gutiérrez move immediately and even integrally beyond mere factual description of the struggle to ethical categories committing the Christian to work within the framework of the struggle for its eventual consummation in the new society? The Bible probably will not intervene against the conclusion of scientific investigation that class struggle exists. But doesn't it intervene at the level of how the Christian ought to relate to the struggle? Doesn't the strategy of the cross place the Christian at odds both with the oppressors and the oppressed who adopt the oppressors' tactics to overcome them? I feel the need here for a more careful analysis of Marxist thought, and in particular to understand just what it means by "scientific" investigation and how the descriptive and normative functions relate in such investigation.

24. H. Richard Niebuhr, *Christ and Culture* (New York: Harper Torchbooks, 1951).

25. Niebuhr describes the way the "Christ-against-culture" and the "Christ-of-culture" models come out at opposite ends of the spectrum on the reason/revelation problem: "Extremes meet and the Christ-of-culture folk are strangely like the Christ-against-culture people, both in their general attitude toward the theology of the church and in the specific theological positions they take. They suspect theology, as radicals do, though for the opposite reason. . . . Like their opponents the cultural Christians tend to separate reason and revelation, but evaluate the two principles differently. Reason, they think (the Christ-of-culture people), is the highroad to the knowledge of God and salvation . . ." (*op. cit.,* p. 110).

26. Gutiérrez admits the ambiguity of historical achievements but insists that such ambiguity does not detract from their salvific character (Gutiérrez, *op. cit.,* p. 177). In the interchange in *Christianity and Crisis* on the "theology of liberation," John Bennett counters the charges of Thomas Sanders (in "The Theology of Liberation: Christian Utopianism," Sept. 17, 1973, issue) of unbridled, unrealistic utopianism in the "theology of liberation." At various points, argues Bennett, Gutiérrez "keeps some Christian realism up his sleeve" (Oct. 15, 1973, 197-198).

27. On the need for biblical theology to restore the authority of the whole canon to recover its current state of crisis, see Brevard S. Childs, *Biblical Theology in Crisis* (Philadelphia: Westminster, 1970), ch. 6, "The Shape of a New Biblical Theology," pp. 91-122.

28. If I understand him correctly, this is one of the main problems José Miguez-Bonino is struggling with in the chapter on "Hermeneutics, Truth and Praxis," in *Doing Theology in a Revolutionary Situation.* But it seems that Miguez also reduces what is applicable to us in the Bible too quickly to merely "germinal events" and certain "directions" towards which these

events point, namely, liberation, righteousness, shalom, the poor, and love. Beyond this, scientific investigation of contemporary reality takes over. Historical correspondence between the N.T. and our situation, in the form of either law or precedent, is rejected (*op. cit.*, p. 103). But doesn't our historical consciousness tend to lead us to "solve" the hermeneutical problem falsely by reducing the universally valid in the Bible to "events"? Doesn't the Bible give us more than a variety of readings on "germinal events" but also a unified (though varied) interpretation of these events, clues as to the authentic self- and world-consciousness of the believer who has been "taken up" into these events (the believer's "union with Christ"), and norms of behavior corresponding to this authentic self- and world-understanding?

29. Miguez-Bonino, *op. cit.*, p. 71. We have already noted that Miguez adopts a similar approach and rejects explicitly the Calvinist's attempt to find historical correspondence between the text and the present in law or the Anabaptist's attempt to find it in precedent (p. 103). See notes 23 and 28, above.

30. *The Politics of Jesus* (Grand Rapids: Eerdmans, 1972). The burden of Yoder's argument is to counter the virtually universal tendency among Christian ethicists and theologians—joined now by Gutiérrez and José Miguez-Bonino—to claim that the Gospels and the N.T. do not provide the substance of Christian ethics in the 20th century. For the "theology of liberation," Marxist social analysis provides the content of Christian ethics. (Recall again Gutiérrez' views on the transformation of reason into political reason, note 23, above.)

31. See, for example, John J. Vincent, "The Para Church: An Affirmative of the New Testament Theologies," *Study Encounter* X, 1 (1974). Vincent finds a pluralism of theologies and underlying models of community in the N.T. and notes the way that diverse contemporary community types "identify" with the portions of the N.T. which provide biblical precedent for their particular model—another version of the "canon within the canon" problem.

32. H. Richard Niebuhr argues compellingly for the need of radicals (Christ-against-culture people) to supplement what they find in the Bible with social and cultural analysis, both in order to determine the rules for governing the countercultural community and to concretize the community's benevolence to the world (*op. cit.*, pp. 69-73).

In a way, Niebuhr's evaluation of the "Christ-against-culture" and the "Christ-of-culture" options anticipates most of the issues we have raised here. His analysis highlights, I believe, most of the points of debate between a "radical evangelical" option and the "theology of liberation." In my view, the "theology of liberation" is best understood as a variant of the "Christ-of-culture" type.

Al Krass speaks to evangelical social activists on this very point: "And here comes the point for evangelical Christians who want to become 'socially involved': we have to recognize the forms of social life have been changing—and enlarging—through history, and that those forms of social life which we find in Scripture are not the only kinds possible. Nor should we expect Scripture to speak—directly—of the kinds of social life in which, as Americans—as members of what is increasingly becoming a 'global village' are involved. That would be to ask of Scripture that it be less than incarnate in the life of the Greco-Roman world—and become something of a 'key' to the understanding of all times and places. This is what Hal Lindsey would have it be. That is to underestimate our own God-given responsibility to be intelligent and perceptive participants in the social orders of our own day, prone to as much ignorance and as many errors of perception and engagement as the people amongst whom we live, and called to the same responsible citizenship as they." ("A Time for Evangelicals to Come to a New Sociological Sophistication," unpublished paper, 1975).

33. Gutiérrez, *op. cit.*, pp. 35, 37, 157. 175-176.
34. *Ibid.*, pp. 36-37. 235.
35. *Ibid.*, pp. 168-169.
36. *Ibid.*, p. 150.
37. *Ibid.*, pp. 153, 168, 177, 198-199, 255.
38. *Ibid.*, p. 268.
39. *Ibid.*, p. 205.
40. *Ibid.*, pp. 108-111.
41. "The creation of the world initiates history, the human struggle, and the salvific adventure of Yahweh. Faith in creation does away with its mythical and supernatural character. It is the work of a God who saves and acts in history; since man is the center of creation, it is integrated into the history which is being built by man's efforts" (Gutiérrez, *op. cit.*, p. 154).
42. Gal. 3:2, 5.
43. When we talk of "proclamation" here we are not necessarily referring to a slavish reduplication of Paul's style of preaching and certainly less of the preaching form of today's popular evangelists. What is needed today is a variety of styles of proclamation which break quite radically from normal evangelistic approaches. What is given here are theological perspectives appropriate to a "non-violent direct action" approach to social change which I would regard as a valid and important proclamation style, and something of an illustration of what I mean by proclamation. The prophets provide excellent models for the variety of approaches to proclamation.
44. J. Andrew Kirk criticizes José Miranda's (*Marx and the Bible*, Orbis) view of justification for its depreciation of the forensic component ("An Initial Exploration into the So-Called 'Theory of Liberation', " *Evangelical Fellow-*

ship of Missionary Studies Bulletin, no. 3 [Oct., 1974], 12-15).

45. I would not regard this transformation as something that happens all at once. In contrast to the popular evangelical notion that regards conversion as primarily a change of mind or crisis experience (and therefore instantaneous) conversion (and repentance) is a process which begins at the point of initial faith. But having said this, it is important to insist that the essential ingredients of real transformation are present from the start (the filling of the Holy Spirit, awareness of the cost of discipleship, commitment to a discipling community, etc.), even though their outworking into life transformation takes place across time.

46. José Miguez-Bonino regards ecclesiology as one of the major weaknesses of the "theology of liberation" as articulated thus far. Miguez Bonino, *op. cit.,* pp. 154, 173, especially pp. 155, 162.

47. These questions are the focus of José Miguez-Bonino's chapter entitled "Church, People, and the Avant-Garde," *ibid.,* pp. 154-173. Of special pertinence to the issue of narrowing the true church to those in ideological or tactical agreement within the struggle, Miguez writes: "We seem to add the religious character of a 'confessing war' to the differences arising from varying analytical, strategic, and tactical positions" (p. 163).

48. This question is the central issue raised about evangelical social action in an unpublished paper by Al Krass, "A Time for Evangelicals to Come to a New Sociological Sophistication." In terms of this dialogue with Gutiérrez, Krass is making a formally identical point to one of the main ones Gutiérrez makes: the necessity of socio-political analysis to supplement biblical revelation in order to be truly obedient to Christ in the present situation. In contrast to Gutierrez, however, Krass finds the "processual" sociological perspective of Durkheim more suited to reality and a biblical view than the sociology of Marx or Mannheim. See note 32 above.

Gutiérrez clearly bends in the direction of saying that true conversion is the *result* of antecedent social change and not the cause. In another sense, however, he views conversion as the act of radical conversion to one's neighbor of which conscious commitment to the class struggle on the side of the oppressed would probably be the purest form. This kind of conversation, of course, *precedes* the structural change. See Gutiérrez, *op. cit.,* p. 205. It seems that a more biblical and less revivalistic concept of conversion moves in the direction of Gutiérrez on this point. But in contrast to Gutiérrez, I would see the social change that precedes conversion happening more in the community of faith than in the society as a whole. The instincts of the "sociology of knowledge" and Marxist epistemology on this point can be quite fully appropriated by evangelicals if more emphasis is placed on conversion as process and the utter necessity of a transformed and transforming community as the nurturing context for the process of conversion.

3. Exodus: The Old Testament Foundation of Liberation

CARL EDWIN ARMERDING*

Introduction

A brief glance at the categories included in the authoritative *Index to Religious Periodical Literature* will show that between 1970 and 1975 the rubric "Liberation Theology" took over as the dominant theme of Western theological thought. Beginning in North America as a Black critique of the dominant White church, and simultaneously in South America as an expression of economic class struggle, the theme of liberation has since been applied to a host of additional movements, most recently (and noisily) to the gay and women's struggles for justice.

In this chapter I will attempt an examination of the theological theme of liberation at the point where it ultimately must be tested, at least by traditional Christian criteria. If liberation theology, as practiced and taught by its adherents, is not a reflection of the theological message of Scripture as understood by a valid hermeneutic, there is little chance of its gaining a hearing in evangelical circles. If, however, there is a valid basis for the new theology, evangelicals need to look carefully and with concern at the challenge being made.

The literature of liberation is by now a rival to John's imagined world-filling account of all that Jesus did and taught. From an Old Testament standpoint, none of the North American liberation move-

---

* Carl E. Armerding, Ph.D., has been serving on the staff of Regent College, Vancouver, B. C., as Associate Professor of Old Testament since 1970. After undergraduate studies at Gordon College, he completed his theological studies at Trinity Evangelical Divinity School, and his doctoral work at Brandeis University. He is the co-editor with Dr. W. Ward Gasque of the 1977 title, *Dreams, Visions, Oracles.*

ments have produced the kind of exegetical theology that would allow a complete critique. Such theological reflection has, however, come forth from a new breed of Latin American theologians, and with the extensive documentation available, in both English and Spanish, a beginning can now be made. Since, however, the biblical basis for liberation is seen as identical by all liberation movements, my chapter will consider briefly North American liberation as well, especially as represented by Black theology.

Liberation theology is basically a response to oppression, or at least what is perceived to be oppression by the theologian. It is not surprising, therefore, that the theme has not arisen in the context of a reasonably secure, self-satisfied North American church. As we will see, the Bible does have much to say about oppression and thus about liberation, but it remains difficult, if not impossible, to feel keenly the sense of liberation until we have felt keenly the sense of oppression. With the liberation theologians, at least those whose voice is considered most authentic, there is invariably an *a priori* perception of the human situation as bondage. In the words of Leander Keck, not himself one of the oppressed, "If [the human situation] is perceived as bondage, God's grace appears as liberation."[1] It is because the authentic perception of liberation can come only from such a milieu that I have chosen to bypass the host of North Atlantic commentaries on liberation and attempt to hear its voice as the voice of those to whom liberation has quite naturally made an appeal. This will include the theological voice of masses of poor people in Latin America as well as the very different voice of American Blacks. If the Latin Americans seem considerably more sophisticated in their theology, that is probably a result of a much older tradition of theological reflection, one that has roots in Augustine as well as Aquinas, and practitioners who have studied with continental economic and social thinkers as well as at Rome's Pontifical Institute.

Preliminary Questions

Hermeneutical Prolegomena

1. *The Nature of Theology.*—Gustavo Gutiérrez, often called the systematic theologian of the movement,[2] describes a shift in the nature

44

and task of theology from the early centuries of the Church onward.[3] Beginning with theology as "wisdom" or meditation on the Bible with personal piety as a goal, the Church later moved to theology as rational knowledge. From the twelfth century onward, culminating in Aquinas, theology established itself as a science, to be studied, catalogued, and propositionally set forth like any other body of knowledge. This kind of scholasticism, although not as formally rejected by the Latin American theologians as its Protestant counterpart has been rejected by North American Blacks, nevertheless is seen as vastly inadequate for today. The new movement stresses the active and existential aspects of the Christian life, a theological task that is seen not so much in what a Christian sets forth propositionally but how he responds to God. The Church's spirituality, visualized in times past as other-worldly, is now seen properly to be apostolic activity, praxis, a Christian presence within history. Theology, as a science, is defined by Gutiérrez as "critical reflection on this *praxis.*"

In a North American response to liberation theology, Frederick Herzog of Duke University Divinity School, points to the same kind of phenomenon. He is one of a growing number of theologians who are increasingly critical of theology, and especially exegetical theology, for neglecting its own socio-economic context and attempting to write theology as if it were detached from the stream of existence.[4] He contends that, as Christianity began among the poor (a contention that may be overly simplistic), the poverty context must serve as an appropriate hermeneutical "application paradigm" in reading the biblical text or doing biblical theology.[5] Theology, then, is not simply an objective science, but a reading of ancient documents with an attempt to understand their context and our context, reflecting on the responses to various practices through the years. Although Herzog does not say so in so many words, he would generally agree with the idea expressed in both Latin American and Black circles, that the church must become either poor or black before it can adequately do or write theology today. Apart from this praxis, the theologian has no meaningful context from which to reflect.

2. *Question of Starting Point.*—It is clear, then, that liberation

hermeneutics would look for a point of departure different from that of classical theological science. In fact, the starting point is seen as radically different from that of not only classical theology but all standard "North Atlantic" (in the case of the Latins) or "White" (in the case of the Blacks) theology. It is a situational hermeneutic, demanding that the reality of the oppression, as determined by socio-economic and political study, be the basis for any theology. In Latin America, this reality is described as an economic and cultural domination of the masses by forces of dehumanization. These forces include internal oppressors like the small class of landholders and industrialists, but even more dominant is the all-pervasive structure of the developed world with its multinational corporations, resource extraction and economic strangulation.[6] Together with the situation as outlined by the social scientists, is seen a new realization on the part of oppressed peoples that they can alter their destiny. Any theology that doesn't consider these two factors will be doomed, and indeed, for the liberation theologians, these facts form the starting point.

The agenda is thus set, but before moving to how the Bible is used to respond to these conditions, I should mention the political stance of most Latin liberationists, as it clearly informs their reading of the text. Rejecting the whole development (*desarrollo*) mentality and especially the "-ism" which development has become for the Third and Fourth World's oppressors (*desarrollismo*), the Latin theologians like Gutiérrez, Rubem Alves, Hugo Assmann, and José Miranda have generally concluded that some form of Marxist critique of society must be accepted as valid. Viewing their own continent as locked into a permanent dependence role,[7] they see no alternative but to accept the inevitability of some form of dialectic that identifies the oppressed and the oppressors in terms that will be meaningful to Latins. That this dialectical analysis of the class struggle, as outlined by Marx, often is assumed as universally valid and scientifically beyond criticism is one of the limiting factors in the method of Latin liberation theology.[8] Just how limiting it is will be seen in our analysis of José Miranda's book, *Marx and the Bible,* probably the best exegetical treatment of Old Testament texts from a liberation perspective. The approach to many texts is severely colored by the author's socio-political rigidity, making what could be a very strong case less than fully applicable to a situation of oppression where the lines do not fall into a workers vs. capitalists confrontation. Any ideology that fails to deal with the structure of oppression (i.e., capitalism) is seen as a preservation of the status quo and therefore opposed to liberation. The same tendency to absolutize a particular social situation is seen in Black liberation theology, where the racial conflict in the contemporary U.S. society determines who can talk about liberation and in what terms. James Cone's earlier work, *A Black Theology of Liberation*,[9] is critical of Karl Barth for starting with Jesus rather than the societal situation, and even goes so far as to claim that Whites cannot, by definition, understand the theology of a book like Exodus.[10]

Much more could be said about starting point and method, particularly in the area of church and society, but it would not serve the purpose of this study. Gutiérrez, in forcing the issue beyond the traditional categories of church and society, in effect blurs the distinction between special and general revelation, with the result that both biblical and ecclesiastical proclamation become less normative. Any reading of Scripture, then, must take its categories from the way it interacts with the progress of history, in a world where the church's voice is no longer heard as a unique, divine Word.

How then is Scripture actually used in liberation theology? In many liberation theologians, particularly of the modern North American variety, Scripture finds relatively little place. Rosemary Reuther's *Liberation Theology*[11] passes over the subject in comparative silence. James Cone, in his *Black Theology of Liberation*,[12] draws inspiration from various allusions to liberation in Scripture, but no attempt is made at real exegesis. However, in what seems to be a significant move back toward a more traditional view, Cone states in his 1975 work, *The God of the Oppressed,* that, although the starting point remains Black experience,

> In God's revelation in Scripture we come to the recognition that the divine liberation of the oppressed is not determined by our perceptions but by the God of the Exodus, the prophets and

Jesus Christ, who calls the oppressed into a liberated existence. Divine revelation *alone* [his italics] is the test of the validity of this starting point. And, if it can be shown that God as witnessed in the Scriptures is not the Liberator of the oppressed, then Black theology would either have to drop the "Christian" designation or choose another starting point.[13]

Among the Latin American theologians, Gutiérrez and most others refer liberally to Scripture. However, the method used, as we shall observe, usually makes the contemporary historical situation normative and relegates the biblical event to the status of a model from which certain principles may be derived, usually by a loose analogy.[14] José Miranda, sensitive to the charge, specifically dissociates himself from "finding parallels between the Bible and Marx," claiming instead, "Our method will be the most rigorous and scientific exegesis."[15] Without a doubt Miranda, almost alone amongst his peers, *has* devoted himself to exegesis. It is difficult to escape the conclusion, however, that his exegesis again is conditioned more by his starting point (a rigid dialectic) than by the canons of biblical theology. *Marx and the Bible* is, nevertheless, a praiseworthy example of liberation concern with its biblical roots.

Salvation as the Key to Biblical Theology

The reigning Old Testament theologian in liberation theology clearly is Gerhard von Rad. Certainly his emphasis on "salvation-history" or God acting within history has found a warm response amongst a group whose basic world perception is oppression. Salvation as liberation is, for Gutiérrez, "the central theme of the Christian mystery." But there is probably another reason for von Rad's popularity. Salvation, as proclaimed by liberation theologians, usually is seen working *outside* of the context or boundaries of a covenant people; hence the understandable reticence to tie the theology too closely to any scheme like that proposed by Walther Eichrodt which unified the Old Testament under the rubric of covenant.

While it is clear, following von Rad, that Exodus must be the starting point for a theology of salvation-history, liberation theology has also been anxious to "recover" the doctrine of creation. Creation, it is affirmed, is the first salvific act, God struggling with human existence,[16] but it is more than that. Creation provides the anthropocentric base for the humanistic thrust of a relatively world-centered theology, and this seems to be at least a part of its appeal. Although Gutiérrez can see the Exodus as the model for a human-centered political salvation, he resorts to the creation narratives as the foundation stone for *man's* crowning role in all subsequent events.[17] Thus, the theology of liberation draws its salvation model from the experience of Exodus, but its anthropology from Genesis 1. How the two are tied together, and the role of other biblical themes, such as covenant and eschatology, will be examined in turn.

Exodus: The Foundation of Old Testament Theology
In Black Theology

James Cone, whose earlier books set the tone of Black theology, has few references to Exodus, but it is clear how he is using that book. Exodus is liberation, the first of God's mighty acts.[18] Although indebted to von Rad (and a host of Negro spirituals) for the basic idea, Cone is fairly straightforward in rejecting the division into multiple theologies that marked von Rad's *magnum opus*. The Exodus event is revelation, that is, it was in the Exodus that God was "tearing down old orders and establishing new ones. . . . God reveals that he is the God of the oppressed, involved in their history, liberating them from bondage."[19] In an interesting departure from his Latin American brethren, Cone has no problem with incorporating covenantal theology into his views on salvation. The Covenant Code (Exodus 21–23) with its humane legislation is considered an integral part of the Exodus experience,[20] while the Sinaitic covenant itself is called "the agreement between Yahweh and this people that he would not cease his liberating activity."[21] The Exodus itself is seen as "political emancipation," in support of which warrior and victory imagery of the Song of the Sea (Ex. 15) is cited.[22] Sin is "a refusal to acknowledge the sign of the Exodus *and* the covenant as God's liberating activity."[23]

An intriguing question arises when one realizes the contrast between Cone and the Latin Americans in their respective attitudes

49

toward covenant. It is precisely at this point that Gutiérrez and Miranda, with their rejection of the "dual planes" of divine activity (i.e., church and world) are uncomfortable. The people of God, for them, has lost any real sense of particularity, and the idea that God works through a covenant seems almost offensive. This is much more explicit in Miranda, but fits well with the theological scheme and world-centered salvation doctrine of the entire movement. By contrast, the salvation Cone envisages in Black theology is *precisely* a covenant theology. Black is the color of covenant and only Black people are in it. This is particularism to the ultimate degree, although in fairness it should be said that Cone's covenant people are born not of an ethnic superiority (i.e., racism) but rather by the oppressive activity of the White majority. He does not elaborate on the parallel fact of Israel's birth in adversity, but here is a line that could be followed with considerable fruitfulness.

Of course, to reduce American history to a basic confrontation between the White power structure and the Black sufferer is simplistic. Nothing is said of individual sinfulness in Black men and relatively little mention is made of individual righteousness in Whites. But, on the model of the Exodus, such an omission is not inadmissible. It was the corporate covenant people which was redeemed, not every member of which was righteous by any means. But unlike Exodus, Cone romanticizes the state of the people and makes little mention of the requirement in Exodus (4:31) that the people must believe in God and worship Him as a prelude to redemption. All in all, Black theology, as represented by James Cone, is considerably more simple in its approach to Scripture than the theology of Latin America. The parallels with Scripture are straightforward, there is almost no ideological base, and hardly any recourse is made to the subtleties of biblical criticism.

In Latin American Theology

Protestant and Roman Catholic theologians agree on the Exodus as the central focus of the biblical message. Rubem Alves, often called the prophet of the movement, even argues that any and all speaking of God derives from this experience, calling the Exodus "the centre which is the principle of organization of the whole biblical language."[24]

Liberation, as a theological category, is merely a footnote to historical events, events which, Alves would claim as a Christian, were not themselves created by man. In the last statement Alves places himself closer to Christian theology than Marxism, although he, like others, sees man now having a fair degree of autonomy.

Probably most representative of the movement is the Peruvian priest, Gustavo Gutiérrez, whose book, *A Theology of Liberation,* while not the most complete treatment of the subject, is probably the most succinct.[25] Here it may be helpful to summarize a few points. As we have seen, "salvation" is the basic notion of Old Testament theology, but for Gutiérrez salvation is not the quantitative design to go forth to all the nations converting the heathen. Rather, it is a qualitative enterprise. Salvation embraces all of human reality and will lead not to a post-historical kingdom of God. Rather, it is achieved in "the communion of men with God and the communion of men among themselves." It is Christ, at the center of God's salvific design who, "by his death and resurrection transforms the universe."[26] This salvation is intrahistorical and all categories in which eschatology is made to transcend history are rejected.[27]

The salvation Gutiérrez envisages does, however, embody an eschatology. The very promise of the Exodus and covenant orients all history toward the future, but the future described by Gutiérrez has derived its categories more from Marxist dialectic than from the Bible. The task of theology and Church is to be engaged, along with others of a more secular mold, in bringing about the salvation first experienced in the Exodus and which entered a decisive stage in the radically incarnational Christ-event. This will include denouncing all injustices, "conscientizing" people to realize that liberation is possible, and identifying in life and work as the poor, as well as changing internal structures and attitudes which are part of the oppression.[28]

Turning specifically to Gutiérrez' use of Scripture, we find first a hermeneutical principle that is basic to all uses of the Old Testament. Whereas traditional Christianity has consistently spiritualized the Old Testament promises, Gutiérrez argues that their intensely political and material context must be retained.[29] Not, of course, that Gutiérrez has any direct interest in or feels any direct identification with a continuing Israel today. Rather, the political nature of the removal of slaves from Egypt is retained as a temporal historical reality, a reality which has meaning for us in the political release of the captive working class from its multinational oppressor. It is Christ who gives the Old Testament promises a contemporary significance, as it is he who "opens new perspectives by catapulting history forward, forward toward total reconciliation."[30]

Although Exodus is the central theme of the Old Testament, Gutiérrez does not give an extensive examination of the passages involved. In fact, his first reference to the subject (other than to quote a Methodist document) comes on page 153, after an extensive discussion of the nature of salvation in the world and church of Latin America. But his method is illustrated in an apparently approving quotation from Karl Marx[31] comparing the Jews in the desert to the present generation. Both, said Marx, have new worlds to conquer and "must perish to give room to the men who are to live in the new world." It is the loose analogy, as hermeneutical method, that predominates, though the basic theology is reasonably settled prior to his approach to the text.

Further use of Exodus seems to concentrate on the theme itself rather than a consideration of its details, with special attention given to how the rest of Old Testament theology can be subsumed under the rubric of political liberation. While the Exodus event is seen as the "true source" of the theme, "Deutero-Isaiah's" well-known parallel in the return from exile is called the "best witness" to the Exodus, along with certain Psalms (74, 89, 93, 135, 136).[32] The conditions of the Israelites in Egypt are recounted (slavery, repression, alienated work, humiliation, and an enforced birth control policy) and the response of the Israelites to their own liberation (initially too alienated to listen and later murmuring for a return to slavery) is seen as a model for an unresponsive populace in an industrial world.[33] Moses' task was the "conscientizing" of the people: that is, he had to awaken in them a hatred for oppression and a realization that they could shape their own destiny.

The Exodus itself is seen as having as a goal "a society free from misery and alienation"[34] and the fact that the religious or covenant event of holy nationhood is the context "gives the Exodus its meaning." But covenant for Gutiérrez is not the calling out of a particular people, but rather "a movement which led to encounter with God."[35] It is at this point where Gutiérrez, although affirming the covenant doctrine, effectively denies the role of particular nationhood and structure, preferring instead a purely relational and general "encounter" theology, a point which does only partial justice to the role of covenant in Israel.

The element of human participation in the Exodus forms a strong sub-theme in Gutiérrez' treatment of the subject. While Creation is seen as the first of God's redemptive acts (despite the anthropocentric nature of the texts), Exodus adds "the need . . . for man's active participation in the building of society." It is "the desacralization" of social praxis, which from that time on will be the work of man.[36] Perhaps here, as much as anywhere, we see the problem of an *a priori*: the biblical Exodus, no less than the creation, is pictured as the work of a sovereign God. The Mosaic admonition, "Stand still and see the salvation of the Lord" (Ex. 14:13), better marks the process than talk of "desacralization" and human creation of a new order. An American Catholic theologian, using the Exodus event likewise as a paradigm for salvation, seems closer to the mark when he writes "The power of Yahweh is interposed in such a way that the persons saved need do nothing."[37]

The concept of God as revealed in Exodus follows fairly standard lines. The "I AM" formula, so frequently used in Exodus, is linked to God's active presence within history rather than to some Greek notion of an ahistorical essence.[38] God's presence is further defined by the symbol of the ark (He is mobile but near), the temple (a complex symbol), and finally passages like I Kings 8 and the prophets, which project a vision of universality.[39] The social legislation of the Book of the Covenant (Ex. 21–23), Deuteronomy, and Leviticus is cited as generally liberating, although no serious attempt is made to study the laws.[40]

An extended section discusses the way creation and exodus (salvation) fit together. Again, following the lead of von Rad, creation is affirmed as an act of God "within history."[41] Indeed, it is "the creation of the world which initiates history, the human struggle, and the salvific adventure of Yahweh."[42] "Faith in creation does away with mythical and supernatural character. It is the work of a God who saves and acts in history; since man is the center of creation it is integrated into the history which is being built by man's efforts."[43] This total desacralization of not only creation but all of redemption-history as well, although seen by these followers of von Rad as a repudiation of primitive doctrines of nature-myth, is really a reduction of a biblical "mythology," which includes the supernatural and supra-historical, to an alien humanistic, secular view of history. This, it may be argued, is demanded by the times we live in or the world-view of the reader, but it is difficult to find in any recension of the Penta-teuch a model for the process.

The Exodus itself is viewed as the great turning-point in the matur-ing process. The dominion over the earth, before the Exodus theology arose, was presumably subordinated to some variety of mythological pagan manipulation of nature. In the Exodus we have "Moses' medi-ation of this self-creation" concept (that is, the idea that all history and work must be done for the good of man), allowing all later men to rise above the mythology of earlier times.[44] The Exodus, then, becomes the paradigm by which creation itself is understood. The problem with more primitive ways of understanding creation, accord-ing to Gutierrez, is that they saw the world in mythological terms, and in myth neither man nor nature controls its own destiny. Political liberation, which explains and interprets nature-creation theology, by contrast ties the two (the natural and social) together as one order. The work of man is the transformation of nature, ridding himself of alienated structures while freeing creation from its bond-age to myth[45]

A second Latin American liberation theologian, José Miranda, is by no means as influential as Alves, Assmann, or Gutiérrez, but should be considered here as an example of serious exegetical theological work. Miranda, like Gutiérrez, is influenced by von Rad and sees liberation as the basic theme. His work is heavily influenced also by studies in theology and economics, as well as years of social action amongst the Mexican working class. The subtitle of his book, *Marx and the Bible,* is "A Critique of the Philosophy of Oppression" and reveals the author's general attitude toward the subject.

The volume in question is a gold mine of theological-exegetical treasure, despite a strong prior commitment to class ideologies that color too many of Miranda's conclusions. At last we have a liberation theologian who speaks more of the language of biblical studies and who is still at home in his Hebrew Bible. At this point it will be impossible to consider all of the matters raised or developed, but I would like to mention a few which illustrate the author's method.

Overshadowing all else is Miranda's intensely held conviction that *mišpaṭ,* which he defines as social justice, salvation of the poor, is a basic datum of the Old Testament.[46] His analysis of the subject is thorough, though tortuous, concluding with the idea that even the last judgment of Jesus and Paul de-emphasizes the action of judging (Greek: *diakrino*) in favor of the result which is justice (Greek: *dikaiosune*). The goal then of all history is justice for the poor, a conclusion which, except for its failure to deal with the supra-historical character of the fulfillment, is not inconsistent with the gospel narratives.

Going back to the Exodus narratives, Miranda takes as a point of departure the need to separate out the various documents and traditions, although his dependence on the Documentary Hypothesis is subordinated to his use of the History of Traditions concept. His thesis is relatively simple, although the means used to develop it is not: whether following the Documentary approach or determining the history of various traditions, the theme of justice for the poor marks the earliest pre-covenantal strata of the Old Testament.

With regard to the Yahwist, such passages as Exodus 2:11-20, 3:7-9, and 9:27 are exegeted with reference to the concern for justice shown by both God and Moses.[47] What is surprising is not that justice appears in the account, but Miranda's contention that none of this early "J-document" material reflects the influence of the covenant doctrine, making them instead a reflection of God's most basic universal concern for all poor.[48] In light of the use of the "my people" formula in 3:7 (a basic covenantal term) and the similarity of that section to the plainly covenantal section in 2:23-25, I wonder if the conclusion is not, even based on Miranda's presuppositions about documents, forced. Does any tradition of the Exodus narrative separate God's general concern from His concern expressed on behalf of His own people? Perhaps of more lasting interest is the point from Exodus 9:27 contrasting "the evil" (*harasaʻ*) Egyptians with God as "the righteous one (*hazzadiq*), language echoed not merely in the Sodom and Gomorrah story (Gen. 18:17-33), but in the more universal wisdom literature as well.

Turning to another line of critical thought, Miranda concurs with Martin Noth in separating radically the traditions which he calls "Exodus-libertarian"[49] from the traditions Noth assigned to Mt. Sinai. Clearly the latter do contain covenantal material, and the concern for justice in the Decalogue or any of the Sinai material is understandable in that context. But, so it is argued, the Exodus tradition in its earliest form knew nothing of Sinai or covenant and thus of covenant concern. Miranda's argument turns on (1) what materials are to be included in the Exodus block, and (2) is there evidence for a non-covenantally conditioned concern for justice in those materials? In a sharp break with Noth, Miranda argues for inclusion of the Book of the Covenant (Ex. 21–23) in the Kadesh-Exodus tradition.[50] Within the Book of the Covenant, Miranda finds a collection of *mišpaṭim* (Ex. 21:1, "these are the ordinances. . . ."), a proof that these old laws of basic justice are to be seen as expressing pre-covenantal ideas of God's justice. In a conclusion to the section,[51] Miranda summarizes the evidence for driving the intense social and ethical concerns of Yahweh back to the earliest thread of Israelite tradition. There is, then, little need for recourse to some later prophetic innovation to explain the concern.

The above is only a sample of Miranda's work, but perhaps it will be enough to show how one modern Roman Catholic liberation theologian has utilized all of the modern tools of biblical criticism, alongside of his social ethics and economic theory, to prove his point from Scripture. If the argument is not entirely convincing, and few Old Testament scholars will find it fully satisfactory, it does illustrate a concern for scriptural support that is a commendable part of much of liberation theology.

Summary and Critique

There are many points at which a critique of liberation theology might be directed, but a general critique has been undertaken elsewhere. As an exegete I would like simply to express a few thoughts on the matters of starting point and method.

Starting Point

Although many have realized in recent years that pure objectivity is a myth, and fruitful studies are being conducted on the ways in which our personal and societal backgrounds structure our views of reality, we must still avoid the relativizing tendency inherent in a method which begins with any culturally or historically conditioned set of circumstances and then fits its exegesis into that. In the case of both Latin and Black liberation movements the theology of the Old Testament is tied to a perception of reality which certainly does not apply equally to other times and places. Even the socio-political analysis of the times and places in question might be challenged; indeed, there are many Latins who are not Marxists and Blacks who do not see it as Cone does. The same could be said of women's movements. The problem, of course, is that we all tend to come out of our exegetical house pretty much where we have gone in, whereas the real task of exegesis is to illuminate the text in its own setting. Building on this the theologian must recognize that the view of reality incorporated in his sources often cuts across his contemporary perceptions. He must respond to that source as his own understanding would direct, but he cannot substitute his own perceptions for those of his source and call the result exegesis. Biblical theology, if it ultimately forces exegetical reconstructions into forms alien to the text and its world, has become just as guilty of proof-texting as was classical dogmatics.

In liberation theology, the starting-point is clearly situational, but what of its method? It seems to me that, as a broad hermeneutical principle, the concept of loose analogy between the Exodus-salvation event and the contemporary oppression-liberation struggles is dominant. No real attempt is made to allegorize the biblical events; there are simply too many points at which the experience of slaves of the Late Bronze Age are not paralleled by any of our twentieth-century phenomena. Rather, there is seen in the Exodus, and various ways of remembering and celebrating that event, a kind of inspirational paradigm that informs and inspires our own struggle.

Theological Methodology

Hopefully, the coming years will see more fruitful work on this aspect of theological methodology. In Old Testament studies scholars like G. E. Wright, G. Mendenhall, and B. S. Childs have suggested some new directions, but a full and reflective study of the subject has yet to emerge. That several of the Latin liberationists have given their attention to the Old Testament and its theology can only further the discussion. If their context is not mine, I can still listen to their work to determine why they find in the events of Old Testament history the meaning they do. But I am convinced that we still need a considerable effort in the direction of a valid and more universally applicable hermeneutic than we have been given. The problem is still that of Alice in Wonderland. Events, no less than words, can come too easily to have whatever meaning we give them; neither more nor less!

Notes

1. Leander Keck, *A Future for the Historical Jesus* (Nashville: Abingdon Press, 1971), p. 101.
2. Orlando Costas, *The Church and Its Mission* (Wheaton, Ill.: Tyndale House, 1974), p. 221ff, n. 4.
3. Gustavo Gutiérrez, *A Theology of Liberation* (Maryknoll: Orbis Books, 1973), chap. 1.
4. Frederick Herzog, "Liberation Hermeneutic as Ideology Critique," *Interpretation* XXVIII (Oct., 1974), 387-403.
5. *Ibid.,* 399ff.
6. See the opening economic-political analysis by both G. Gutiérrez (*op. cit.,*

chap. 2) and José Miranda, *Marx and the Bible* (Maryknoll: Orbis Books 1974), chap. 1. There is a sympathetic critique by Costas, *op. cit.*, chap. 10.
7. Gutiérrez, *op. cit.*, pp. 84ff.
8. See René Padilla, "Current Religious Thought," *Christianity Today*, 18 (November 9, 1973), 69ff.
9. James Cone, *A Black Theology of Liberation* (Philadelphia: J. B. Lippincott, 1970), p. 51.
10. *Ibid.*, p. 53.
11. Rosemary Reuther, *Liberation Theology* (New York: Paramus, 1972).
12. Cone, *op. cit.*
13. James Cone, *The God of the Oppressed* (New York: Seabury Press, 1975), p. 88.
14. Cf. Costas' critique, *op. cit.*, pp. 240ff.
15. José Miranda, *op. cit.*, p. xvii.
16. Costas, *op. cit.*, p. 233.
17. Gutiérrez, *op. cit.*, p. 158.
18. Cone, *A Black Theology of Liberation*, pp. 63ff.
19. *Ibid.*, p. 18.
20. *Ibid.*, p. 64.
21. *Ibid.*, p. 188.
22. *Ibid.*, p. 94.
23. *Ibid.*, p. 187.
24. R. Alves, "Theology and the Liberation of Man," *New Theology No. 9*, ed. by Martin E. Marty and Dean G. Peerman (New York: The Macmillan Company, 1972), p. 237.
25. For a thorough critique, based largely on Gutiérrez, see Costas, *op. cit.*
26. Gutiérrez, *op. cit.*, p. 149.
27. *Ibid.*, pp. 160ff.
28. *Ibid.*, p. 114.
29. *Ibid.*, p. 166.
30. *Loc. cit.*
31. *Ibid.*, p. 146., n. 3.
32. *Ibid.*, p. 155.
33. *Ibid.*, p. 156.
34. *Ibid.*, p. 157.
35. *Loc. cit.*
36. *Ibid.*, pp. 158ff.
37. John T. McKenzie, *A Theology of the Old Testament* (Garden City, N. Y.: Doubleday, 1974), p. 145.
38. *Ibid.*, p. 165.
39. *Ibid.*, p. 190.
40. *Ibid.*, p. 293.
41. *Ibid.*, p. 153.
42. *Ibid.*, p. 154.
43. *Loc. cit.*
44. *Ibid.*, p. 159.
45. *Ibid.*, p. 173.
46. Miranda, *op. cit.*, pp. 109ff.
47. *Ibid.*, pp. 97ff.
48. *Ibid.*, pp. 88ff.
49. *Ibid.*, pp. 137-150.
50. *Ibid.*, p. 137.
51. *Ibid.*, pp. 149f.

59

4. The Mission of the Church

HARVIE M. CONN*

Hugo Assmann, a Brazilian priest, warns against making the "theology of liberation" a "consumer product to make up for your impotence; don't be spectators of our small achievements, nor project on Latin America an image of compensations; and finally, all of you, each in his own context, enter into the same struggle. . . ."[1] Among other things, Assmann is calling on us to make this "theology" a form of self-dialogue, a form of conscientization, to use the language of Paulo Freire,[2] "the awakening of the Christian conscience."[3]

In that spirit, and assuming the risks it obliges us to take, this chapter will focus on the theology of liberation not primarily as an object of analysis but as a participant in a dialogue of evangelical self-reflection. We propose to listen with as much sensitivity as we can to the questions implicitly and explicitly addressed to evangelical missions practice by the theologians of liberation. To be sure, we will ask if some of those questions are legitimate and properly framed. But our primary purpose will be to see how the fruit of the reflection of men like Gutiérrez and Juan Luis Segundo can serve "as an instrument in the refinement of our own commitment to the Gospel and all that this requires in terms of our commitment."[4]

Danger Signals Calling Us to Listen

There are a number of warnings that underline our need for listening. They are mirrored in the discovery of a young Latin American

---

* Harvie M. Conn, Th.M., Litt.D., currently serves as Associate Professor of Missions and Apologetics at Westminster Theological Seminary, Philadelphia. He began his ministry there in 1972, after twelve years of service as a foreign missionary of the Orthodox Presbyterian Church in Korea. The author of *Contemporary World Theology,* he has recently edited and contributed to the volume, *Theological Perspectives on Church Growth.*

missionary that a Communist friend had made 250 converts to Communism in a year. Another young man who left the church for Communism told him why, in his view, it took so long to win people to Christianity: 'You Protestants are anxious to make people give up drinking and smoking. The Communists are concerned about the relief of suffering and injustice.' "[5]

It is mirrored in the judgments of Dr. Roger Greenway of the Christian Reformed Church. "Thousands of Catholic clerics," he writes, "are asking uncomfortable questions all across Latin America. Injustice, hunger, exploitation, racism, oppression, poverty, infant mortality, and military operations for no visible purpose than to make some men richer cannot remain unanswered and unabated forever. No one can escape the conclusion that most Latin American governments are operated for the benefit, not of the majority of the people, but for the privileged minority."[6] Against that concern, he speaks of "the negligible impact of the evangelical church as a whole on the gradually emerging new society and the isolation of the churches from the totality of human life."[7]

It is mirrored in a Mexico City survey that indicates "the basic moral and social attitudes of evangelicals in Mexico City are not notably different from those of many of their nonevangelical neighbors." "The new life in Christ is commonly interpreted negatively— no smoking, no drinking, no fornicating, no parties—and a sharp line of demarcation is drawn between the 'church' (which represents everything good) and the 'world' (everything bad)."[8] "In general," writes one evangelical observer of the pattern, "thinking Latin Americans have rejected evangelical Christianity as being irrelevant to their countries' problems."[9]

Repeatedly, René Padilla, an awakened evangelical conscience in Argentina, has seen it. "Is not the radical leftist theology itself, at least in part, a reaction against the deadly reduction of the Christian mission that has characterized Latin American Protestantism?," he asked in 1971.[10] "Have we made the Christian faith really *ours* while we limit ourselves to repeating certain formulas worked out in other latitudes?," he asked in 1972.[11] By 1974, his questions have been formed into a strident rebuke in the wake of the collapse of the

61

Allende government in Chile and the sharing of the "common opinion" that his fall was provoked by the encouragement of the United States Department of State. "One does wonder, however, whether the acquiescence on the part of so many evangelical Christians was not due less to ignorance of the facts than to political views leading them to overlook crimes that they would not have overlooked under the Marxist government."[12] The gentle disclaimer in the editorial pages of the same magazine that published his essay would indicate that North American observers have not been looking as long and as concernedly as he has.

Other voices see the same patterns displayed in Latin American theological education. Ross Kinsler, writing of the protestant-evangelical-pentecostal movement, notes that "we preach a message of individual salvation which utterly ignores the social sins, the terrible injustices, and the inhumanity of man to man which are so prevalent. And within the protestant churches themselves there is little that can be called liberating. The local church is not only a refuge from the problems of life; it becomes another oppression enclosing and controlling the life of its members. Standards of behaviour are largely negative and strictly enforced."[13] Less clearly evangelical but no less devastating and directly to the point is the staff paper of the Theological Education Fund. "Dissatisfaction has been widespread among theological educators, especially in the Third World, with regard to the traditional curriculum and method of teaching in the seminaries. They are dissatisfied because they realize that the training is too remote from life, and irrelevant to the concerns and issues of society. . . . What does all of this mean for theological curriculum and teaching? Theological educators will need to struggle hard for an answer. Perhaps to start with, the seminary and Church together should examine the concrete need and content of Christian ministry in the present, local, context and approach afresh the designing of the pattern and style of theological education on that basis. In the meantime, the seminary community itself must take its missionary obligation seriously and exemplify, in some way, through its institutional life, a genuine commitment to liberation, not only in education but also in general, social terms."[14]

What Evangelical Missions Has Said to Latin America

To a greater extent than we usually care to admit, the Latin American "missionary has conceived of his mission to the young Church as reproducing the North American Church of which he is a part. Forms, structures, and functions have been transported *in toto* to a Latin American setting, not as an expression of theological imperialism but as a sincere effort to produce a Church that is biblical and orthodox."[15]

A deep part of that form was structured by the pietist roots of North American evangelicalism. Nurtured especially in the so-called "faith missions," its influence would be particularly strong after the 1930s, when they began to arrive in Latin America in greater numbers. By 1958, out of 5,431 missionaries working in Latin America, Harold Lindsell designates 3,182 as representing this stream.[16]

In the foundations of its past, pietism carried with it a strong focus on the individual's relationship to God, a stress on Christian experience and devotion that sometimes defined itself in terms of a self-discipline which included abstinence from playing cards, dancing, and the theatre, and moderation in food, drink, and dress. Suspicious of the cultural Christianity that characterized the age of reason, pietism's proper fear of the intellectualizing of Christianity sometimes degenerated into an underemphasis of doctrine and theology, reinforced by emphasis on introspection. It did not neglect the expression of that faith in society. Faith for the pietist was the sun, good works were the sun's rays. Schools, orphanages, and other philanthropic organizations were a rich part of its heritage to contemporary evangelical patterns of missions. But these were conceived of as the task of the individual Christian, the fruits of his faith. It did not so much demand a Christian approach to politics or economics and social issues as it demanded that the individual Christian approach politics or economics or social issues. Amelioration, not reformation, was at the heart of that response.

The subsequent history of pietism as it manifested itself in North American mission agencies served to reinforce many of these incipient hangovers from the past. By and large, evangelical missions drew its financial and personnel strength from the growing "middle class" of North America. And from the cultural myths of that class there developed a strong feeling for the identification of Christianity with keynotes of *lessez-faire* capitalism—individual initiative, fear of governmental control of the market, the power of the consumer in social and economic change, the upward mobility of class structures, democracy as the most suitable (biblical) form of government, organization as a key in maximum development, the inevitability of progress, the middle class as the source of change and progress in every society.[17] Pietism's highly individual mood, its ameliorative focus on societal change, its emphasis on the self-discipline of the virtues of moderation, thrift, hard work, only served to reinforce these cultural patterns of understanding and sanction the cultural myths without any fully biblical evaluation of their legitimacy or value.

The effect, according to Samuel Escobar, has been to create "a middle class captivity" of the Latin American evangelical church. And this has cultivated a mentality reluctant to deal with social responsibility. So, "politics is worldly, business is not. Active membership in a labor union is worldly, active membership in an association of real estate owners is not worldly. Giving alms to the poor is acceptable, organizing them to fight the causes of poverty is not acceptable."[18] The gospel in Latin America becomes identified with a middle-class ideology.[19]

Still another reinforcing factor in this emerging reductionism of Latin American evangelicalism has been the Western theological conflict over the "social gospel." Quite properly, the demands of that movement were seen not as adding a new dimension to missions but as destructive of its very heart, a distortion in which the gospel was lost.[20] But this evangelical response, reinforced by pietism's neglect of the social dimensions of the gospel, and the baptism of "middle class" mythology, turned to reaction against the expression of the social dimension of our Christian testimony. And reaction turned to neglect, and retrogression. Church and mission in Latin America did not see the temptation of reducing the gospel by the elimination of any demands for the fruit of repentance by an idolatrous society.

And this has been the danger constantly drawn attention to by the evangelical radicals of Latin America today—the Padillas and the Escobars. Church and mission have fallen into a dualistic reductionism, a form of evangelical dimensionalism which is in danger of presenting "a saving work of Christ without the consequent ethical demands, . . . a Saviour who delivers from the bondage of spiritual slavery but not a model of the life that the Christians should live in the world, a spirituality without discipleship in the daily social, economic, and political aspects of life. . . ."[21] This dimensionalism manifests itself in the polarities drawn by evangelical missions today.

A polarity between proclamation and presence often functions on a pragmatic level within the Latin Church. Nourished by the early years of Protestant history in the continent when the struggle for survival had to be carried on with a very low profile, proclamation in some circles became words and "presence" became pre-evangelism.[22] "In this struggle for survival there was little time for reflection on the theoretical relationship of the church to the hostile social, economic, or political systems under which it existed."[23] In the years particularly since Vatican II, and with the growing size of the Protestant force, the question has remained unresolved among many. Proclamation is often identified now by the left-wing Protestant with proselytism, "brother" evangelizing "brother." And the debates within the World Council of Churches on "Christian presence," involving partly a studied reluctance towards verbalization of the gospel,[24] tend to make the pre-evangelism of presence even further removed, into something resembling pre-pre-evangelism.

Evangelicals as a whole have not altogether been touched by these kinds of bifurcations. The large majority of Latin American Protestants apparently would not admit that Roman Catholicism is a legitimate expression of Christianity and therefore be any less reluctant about evangelism. And by no means have they succumbed to any definition of "presence" that would make it an end, not a means, in preaching the gospel. But the bifurcations remain no less real.

"There has been a tendency in the evangelical church in Latin America to identify social concern with theological liberalism or with spiritual coldness and lack of concern for evangelism."[25] Reinforced by what Escobar terms "the middle class mentality" of the evangelical, it has produced a form of evangelism that defines repentance and a new life in Christ largely in terms of drunkards leaving their alcohol, disobedient children respecting their parents. "We promise the neurotics that they will find spiritual peace and the psychologically disturbed that they will find the fountain of tranquillity. But what does our message have to say to the ones who exploit the Indians, to capitalist abusers, to corrupt government officials who accept bribery, to dishonest politicians? What about the comfortable indifference in our churches toward the suffering of the masses? 'Presidential breakfasts' and meetings with authorities are popular today. Have evangelicals raised a prophetic voice at these?"[26] The effect is to create a theological gap between the Word of the Lord and the world of the Lord.

This can easily be enforced by careless theorization. The suggestions of Harold Lindsell in dealing with the relation of kerygma and diakonia, for example, attempt a solution by a bifurcation between the church and the individual. "Individual Christians, as members of Caesar's kingdom as well as of God's kingdom, should be involved in political and economic affairs insofar as they are competent and have opportunity. But the church as church should engage in works of mercy, including such things as relief for the poor, help for the underprivileged, medical aid for the sick, and education for the illiterate."[27] Remembering the strongly individual focus of pietism, such a position cannot help but enforce an already bifurcated pattern into a two-kingdom theory that moves beyond the church-state polarity of classical Lutheranism to an individual-state polarity.

Still another theoretical option is that suggested by men like Donald McGavran, who would argue that the duty of the church "includes doing justice, loving kindness and walking humbly with God," but the duty of "biblical missions or missionary missions" is evangelism in what he feels to be its classically restrictive sense, proclaiming "Jesus Christ as divine, and the only Saviour" and encouraging "men to become his disciples and responsible members of His church."[28] The polarity remains, constructed now not in terms

66

of individual/society, but in terms of church/mission, discipling/perfecting.[29]

The same polarity reappears in a definition of "spiritual" that finds its meaning, not in contradistinction to the Pauline category of "fleshly" understood as life outside of Christ (Rom. 8:8; Gal. 5:16ff.)[30] but in contrast to life as the material, the seen, the sensate world.[31] So, the Latin American evangelical is said to "have adopted a mentality which holds that everything that surrounds us is 'worldly' and that since it does not contribute anything to a truly 'spiritual' development, it has to be eliminated radically."[32] Molded by an "eschatological escapism," to use Padilla's language, until recent history a persecuted minority, the church has "become somewhat withdrawn into itself. For persecuted Christians it was a haven of rest, a center of fellowship with those of like mind, and a balm to troubled souls. Separation from the world and from worldly practices was the order of the day, not only because of social pressures, but also because of the strict puritanical orientation of many of the evangelical missionaries."[33] The monastic model long set before the Latin evangelical in his culture has itself been transposed into an evangelical monastic mind-set.

By no means is this emerging picture uniform or historically part of the evangelical tradition of Latin America. "Pablo Besson, a Swiss Baptist missionary in Argentina, was a fighter for religious and civil freedom, and his battles took him to the Argentinian Parliament. Evangelical missionaries were active in the fight for religious and civil freedom in Peru. Also in several Latin American countries, evangelicals have been champions of the rights of Indian majorities enslaved by centuries of white domination."[34] Evangelicals were in the vanguard of the agrarian reform in Bolivia, of medical assistance in various parts of the Andes, of the school systems of Argentina, Peru, Mexico, and Cuba, of the fight for the rights of Indians. Evangelicals, both missionary and national, in the past of Latin America have showed great sensitivity to human needs.

But increasingly that picture has been changed. And so, with sadness, it has been noted that today, "many young people in Latin America, who were motivated by the Gospel to love their neighbor and be concerned for justice and freedom in their society, have often become Marxists simply because their churches did not provide biblical instruction about Christian discipleship, or because they were blind to clear demands from the Bible and opportunities and challenges provided by new social situations."[35]

One response to the dilemma has suggested that kerygma be seen as "the primary relationship of the church to the world" and diakonia, Christian social service, be "the secondary relationship."[36] Reminiscent of the suggestion of McGavran, the response flows from a deeply biblical realization that evangelism "is not optional for the church, and there is no evangelism without proclamation. . . . But equally true and biblical is the fact that the gospel is a message that must be lived. . . . The proclamation of the gospel (kerygma) and the demonstration of the gospel through service (diakonia) form an indivisible whole."[37] That whole is rent by speaking of "primary" and "secondary." It is the same separation that defines "the mission of the church" as "preeminently spiritual—that is, its major concern revolves around the nonmaterial aspects of life. . . . Kerygma and service are true yokefellows, but even as in marriage the headship belongs to the husband, so kerygma has ordered priority over service."[38] But it is not ordered priority so much as it is kerygma that serves and service that proclaims. There can be no ordered priority or duality even of a temporal sort, which severs what "Jesus began to do" from what "Jesus began to teach" (Acts 1:1-2). Even the Lausanne Covenant, seeking basically to maintain this wholeness, and acknowledging "Christian presence in the world" as "indispensable to evangelism" still sees "responsible service in the world" as a *result* of evangelism, but not an integral part of it, "both part of our Christian duty."[39] Dualisms are not resolved by dualisms.

Still another area where the polarity of the church's self-understanding appears is the dichotomizing of individual and society, privatization as it were. Christian Lalive d'Epinay, in his classic study of the Pentecostal Church of Chile, charges repeatedly that "Pentecostalism teaches its initiates withdrawal and passivity in sociopolitical matters, limited only by the commandment to be submissive to authority. . . . These components make it in the last analysis a force for order rather than an element of progress, a defender of the status quo and not a promoter of change."[40] Those charges have been challenged properly in many quarters.[41] It is not so much that society is being ignored as it is that the Western ethnotheological focus on the individual, strengthened by the Latin American cultural patterns emphasizing the personal leader as change agent, and authoritarian center in socio-politics,[42] have combined to privatize the agent of social interaction. Thus, in a carefully controlled survey of 341 interviews taken among members of Reformed churches in Mexico (113), Peru (115), and Argentina (112), it was apparent that the Reformed church members could not be said to view themselves as apolitical. They agreed "that the citizen has the obligation to help correct . . . injustices" but rejected "politics as a means to achieve social ends. . . ."[43] They "did accept social responsibilities at a personal level, however. . . ."[44] This tendency might easily be reinforced by the missionary example, the classic evangelical stance, of apolitical involvement in his host country and restraint from actively promoting any one interpretation of how social structures can best be changed.

Evangelical theorizing on this area has not always caught the dangerous role privatization can play in hindering social involvement. Peter Wagner pays no attention to it in his defense of Pentecostal patterns of social participation. He pleads for "meaningful and tangible programs of social service" by the church[45] and warns of a confusion of priorities of God's commands to the church, a theme we have seen him repeat elsewhere. His ultimate criterion seems to be whether it "helps, not hinders, numerical church growth."[46] Part of his reluctance may stem from his theological commitment to a merely future aspect of the kingdom of God, his conviction, often associated with dispensationalism, that "the kingdom of God . . . will not arrive before Christ's second coming."[47] But a large share of the problem comes also from his failure to interact with privatization as a Western ethnotheological import, quite at home in Latin American culture patterns.

In yet another set of dualisms do we see the polarism of evangelical mission ambiguity appear. It is in the dichotomizing of ec-

clesial and humanitarian interests, the strange anomaly observed by
Samuel Escobar of foreign missionaries in some Latin American
countries who spend their lives among the poor or the Indian mi-
norities while "there are hundreds of national graduates who attend
'fundamental' churches but show no concern for their own fellow
countrymen. They have no concern for their material or spiritual
welfare."[48]

The dualism flows from an understanding of the expression of
the Christian faith largely conceived of in terms of participation in
the institutionalized church and its calendar. The role of the Christian as the "new man" (Eph. 4:24), growing to "a mature man"
(Eph. 4:13), being "conformed to the image of his Son" (Rom.
8:29), is not seen as a process of "humanization" into the second
Adam, but "almost absolute submission in the precise observation of
a multiplicity of details, slogans, programs, outlines, schedules of
meetings, etc."[49] Living the Christian life is transposed by the cultural process into living the institutional church life. The cosmic,
humanitarian dimensions of the gospel are reduced to the life of a
church building, biblical humanization into cultural ecclesiology.

What the Theology of Liberation Is Saying to Us

Against the dualistic background of this sacred/secular, spiritual/
material version of Christian missions' "Babylonian captivity," what
does the theology of liberation demand from us?

At its core is the call to praxis, what Gutierrez designates as "a
new way to do theology."[50] The demand is basic enough for Rosemary Reuther to say that "the theology of liberation is not a dogmatic
a priori but a creative reflection upon *praxis.*"[51] The term designates
much more than simply some "reflection on the situation of the believer in the world." It is that which antecedes reflection. It takes
much of its meaning from its use in Karl Marx as the call for response arising out of the historical moment. Man, the aggregate of
his social relationships,[52] is to act in concord with what is to be
the future. It is the call to self-realization in making (or changing)
history, in work, the subjecting and forming of matter. It is formed
out of the need to break with what is, in favor of joining the

struggle for what is to be, the reconciliation of man with himself and with his own powers of production.[53] It is man being man, not when he is meditating, but when he is transforming the objective world freely (*homo laborans*). "If he loses this possibility he loses his humanity."[54]

In the theological process constructed by Gutiérrez, praxis is that on which theology critically reflects. Theology thus becomes "the fruit of a confrontation between the Word accepted in faith and historical praxis,"[55] "man's critical reflection of himself, his own basic principles."[56] But again, even in the theological process, praxis does not lose its Marxist connotations of participation in the class struggle to bring about the creation of the new man. Hugo Assmann warns against idealizing by such an abstraction "the ambivalent reality of man's historical activity. . . . Theological reflection, in short, must take its place where any process of self-understanding has to be—in the real course of historical events. That applies both to interventions on the international scale and to the detailed working out of political strategy and tactics on the basis of a particular situation."[57] Theology must be rooted in the contextual praxis, rooted in the human and therefore political dimension.

It is this fear of abstraction that fills the pages of liberation theology books with sharp criticisms of even Europe's political and revolutionary theologians. With such thinking it shares many things.[58] But it sees also a fear in revolutionary theology's unwillingness to name directly the mechanism of domination.[59] Johannes Metz is castigated for distinguishing between the task of theology and ethical politics. The task of theology must detect the critical aspects of faith in relation to historical praxis, and ethical politics must deal directly with the question of praxis. Such a distinction is inconceivable and unacceptable to liberation theology.[60]

At the heart of this kind of judgment is the Marxist critique of idealism and its lack of historical realism. Its questions are not touching the real in its dialectical conflict. Reality is idealized into an apolitical accommodation to the pragmatism of man in consumer societies. In the same vein, the theologians of secularization are criticized for concentrating only on the desacralization of nature and the man-nature relationship. They have not taken into account the man-machine relationship in its power-domination expression.[61] On the contrary, the theology of liberation has to face the power problem with historical, dialectic realism. Thus theology must flow from praxis. Theology must be committed not to the abstract conceptions and objective sources of the North Atlantic constructions, the "ideology of the status quo," but to an "ideology of struggle."

In the same vein, liberation theology distances itself from theologians like Rahner, Küng, and others whose concentration is "almost exclusively on action inside the Church, the general concern of postconciliar reformism." Liberation theology, with its insistence on praxis as a *locus theologicus,* "shifts the emphasis toward liberating action, in a strongly political sense, in the context of the conflict situation of the world today."[62] Even these movements do not escape the charge of a "fundamentalism of the Left."[63]

How will evangelical missions respond to this call for praxis? In too many articles, he has not responded at all, either by way of seeing praxis as the heart of the liberation critique,[64] or by way of analysis when he does.[65] He must begin by recognizing that there seems to be a difference among liberation theologians as to the extent and intensity of their commitment to a distinctively Marxist social analysis in the use of the term.[66] And with humility he must admit that "theology (and exegesis) is inevitably influenced by the ideological, cultural, and socio-political values and commitments of the interpreter/theologian."[67] Liberation theology reminds us of the myth of "objective" exegesis and the triumphalist tendency to equate theological construction with the revelation of God. The doctrine of inerrancy must be preserved as a biblical given, but even it is not a final refuge against theological distortion by those who may hold it.

It is particularly in the equation of praxis with the social-economic spheres that evangelicals must strongly resist the call of liberation theology. Whether modified or not, its core remains Marx's demand for man's self-creation in his productive labor. His definition of productivity as human self-externalization, as self-objectification, has been transposed into liberation categories of oppressor/oppressed. And that definition bears within itself "the power to subject to itself the whole of reality and to bring it under its own humanizing regime.[68] The roots of that definition lie not in a biblical view of man but in the Renaissance view of man as one who regenerates himself by his own powers. There are no limits to the "historical expansion-power of the Self in the reality in which we are placed."[69] The rooting of praxis in economic struggle is a grandiose example of that form of "immanence philosophy" in which the non-Christian "must needs find the ground and integration of reality *within* the created order."[70] In this case, his Archimedean point becomes economics, and reality is constructed around that central idol. A legitimate part of the creation has been deified into an integrating "ultimate concern" that ruptures the meaning-fulness of the creation in its triune Creator. The result is a worse form of abstractionism than liberation theology itself fears, the abstraction of the economic spoke of creation from its hub in the Creator.

Having said this, the evangelical must also hear in the liberation call for praxis a call for repentance, a reminder of the "unpaid bills of the church" in Latin America, an opportunity to rectify the polarity between proclamation and presence we have sketched earlier. Is there in our evangelical praxis an aloofness from social analysis and interaction that amounts to a de facto "fundamentalism of the Right"? Does our concern for the purity of the proclamation of the gospel incorporate too little of Gutiérrez' concern that love be concrete? Is the popularity of Marxism as a theological construct in Latin America not the emergence of the scornful epithet, "poor talkative little Christianity"? Has the evangelical's proper insistence on the gospel as "truth in itself" been so absolutized as to disconnect it from the historical "now" of truth-in-action? Is our concept of theology too heavily influenced by a Cartesian rationalistic methodology so that we tend to lose sight of theology as "simply the application of Scripture to all areas of human life."[71] Will the church growth school's distinction between "discipling and perfecting" into separate spheres of church-mission responsibility run us again into the risk of what Knapp calls "an introversion of concern" and thus deeper into what liberation theology warns against, a failure to demonstrate sufficiently the other-directedness of the love of Christ? Do the traditional evangelical formulations on kerygma and diakonia adequately serve to define either evangelism or service?

All these questions are mandates for the development of a more adequate, biblical praxiology of faith, an orthopraxis hinted at in the popular phraseology of Francis Schaeffer, the practice of the truth. Such a praxiology cannot begin simply by denying the existence of truth "of itself,"[72] but neither can it end by affirming adherence to truth as simply an intellectual matter, "an ordering of biblical data, . . . a process of theory construction from the facts of the Bible."[73] The former can involve a surrender of truth to a pseudo neo-orthodox activism, the latter can isolate truth from the practice of radical obedience. The one alternative forgets a steward's responsibility over the deposit of truth Paul calls "the mysteries of God" (I Cor. 4:1), the "tradition" he had "received" (I Cor. 15:3; Gal. 1:12), the other forgets that repentance "leads to the knowledge of truth" (II Tim. 2:25), that by our walk "we do not the truth" (I John 1:6). An evangelical praxiology must never seek by its theory or practice to promote a truth isolated from immersion in the world and in the historical process. Neither may it be content with the promotion of truth or faith "as basically its practice, its working out in history."[74]

Liberation theology calls us to practice what we preach, to be "letters . . . known and read by all men" (II Cor. 3:2), to "prove what the will of God is" by the "living and holy sacrifice" of our lives lived out before God (Rom. 12:1-2). Evangelical theological method must include a hermeneutic of action, an interaction of living by the Word of the Lord in the world of the Lord. Any mission theorizing which builds, in any way, a wall between the truth of God and the "doing of truth" (I John 1:6) must be discarded as a dualism that rends the seamless robe of kerygma and diakonia. Diakonia is destroyed when it is not contextualized into clothing for the naked, visits to the sick, food for the hungry (Matt. 25:31-46), cups of cold water in the name of Jesus. Kerygma is destroyed when it is confession of "Lord, Lord," by those who practice lawlessness (Matt. 7:21-22). Evangelical praxiology confesses that "without the norm of Scripture (canon), the Christian faith runs the risk of losing itself in the concrete situation, . . ."[75] and that without the concrete situation (hermeneutical context), the Christian faith runs the risk of losing itself in irrelevancy. This is not a call to "consider Scripture a primary frame of reference *together with* the situation."[76] It is a call to consider Scripture a primary frame of reference in confrontation of the situation.

In the face of the evangelical duality of spiritual-material, liberation theology calls also for politicization. Gutiérrez sounds that note very clearly. "To work, to transform this world, is to become a man and to build the human community; it is also to save. Likewise, to struggle against misery and exploitation and to build a just society is already to be part of the saving action, which is moving toward its complete fulfillment. All this means that building the temporal city is not simply a stage or 'humanization' or 'pre-evangelization' as was held in theology up until a few years ago."[77]

This is much more than simply the assertion of "a direct immediate relationship between faith and political action."[78] Such a relationship, argues Gutiérrez, is not possible "except through the effort to create a new type of person in a different society," through the building of a utopia which denounces the existing order and annunciates what is not yet but will be, a different order of things built on a realization of historical praxis. "The Gospel does not provide a utopia for us! this is a human work."[79]

Thus theology must become an activistic articulation of the liberating hope of man, not an abstract definition of eschatological hope, as in Moltmann. Applauded though Moltmann's work may be,[80] it is attacked by liberation theology for running the risk of relegating man to the role of an inactive eschatological spectator.[81] It replaces a Christianity of the Beyond and its tendency to forget the world with a Christianity of the Future and its danger of "neglecting a miserable and unjust present and the struggle for liberation."[82] Theology must be politicized, it must be "part of the process through which the world is transformed. It is theology which is open—in the protest against trampled human dignity, in the struggle against the plunder of the vast majority of people, in liberating love and in the building of a new, just and fraternal society. . . ."[83]

75

Against this background, one is called by liberation theology to affirm "the positive relation between God's kingdom and man's historical undertaking," "a call to engage ourselves actively in the latter. The gospel invites and drives us to make concrete historical options and assures them eschatological permanence insofar as they represent the quality of human existence which corresponds to the Kingdom."[84] The kingdom is God building His rule "from and within human history in its entirety. . . . Man's response is realized in the concrete arena of history with its economic, political, ideological options."[85] No longer can the *political* character of this history" of the kingdom in the Scriptures be seen "almost exclusively in terms of the moral and religious life of the individual"[86] or identified, as Augustine did it, "with the hierarchical, the pious, or the orthodox Church."[87] Such discontinuities between kingdom and general history, between the building of the kingdom and action on sociopolitical structures must be abandoned for a continuity with the world. "The Kingdom is not an object to be known through adumbrations and signs that must be discovered and interpreted but a call, a convocation, a pressure that impels. History, in relation to the Kingdom, is not a riddle to be solved but a mission to be fulfilled."[88] The divine initiative of the kingdom is that action of God within history and in historical terms which opens history toward the promise.

In all this, the evangelical must see more than merely a new formulation of the "political dimension of faith." Assmann fears the ambiguity of simply speaking "of the political 'consequences' of faith, since this gives a false impression that it is possible to live a life of faith in isolation. . . ."[89] It is rather a re-definition of faith as "no more or less than man's historical activity (which is essentially political)."[90] And it is that politico-history which structures our understanding of the kingdom of God. It is that history which becomes the mission of the kingdom, the announcement of the presence of the love of God in the "historical becoming of mankind." The vertical dimension to the kingdom tends to be sublimated in the historical now and the struggle of the oppressed for liberation. The eschatological dimension is "realized" in the hermeneutic of history's economic, social, political concretization. The "spiritual" dimension is ideologized into man's bringing to judgment the socio-political reality.

Can the evangelical hear anything more than this? Can he hear the charges of an individualization of the kingdom that sees only an individualistic Jesus concerned merely with the salvation of individuals? Can he hear the outcry against making a kingdom not of this world into a kingdom not of any world at all? Can he hear the anger at a spiritualization of the kingdom into a kingdom shorn of political, social, economic implications and power? Can he hear the fear of an "eschatological escapism" that withdraws the kingdom so far into the future it cannot touch the present? that makes the kingdom a waiting room for the rapture? a kingdom so far "within" it never appears without? a pietistical world-flight into other-worldly irrelevance?

The evangelical response must begin with an underlining of the God-centered character of the kingdom, rule by Jesus, the King of kings. "The heavenly *polis* does not lack a political form, but the form of the kingdom is *theopolitical,* the saving rule of God."[91] The announcement of the coming of the kingdom is the announcement of the coming of the King (Matt. 3:2) to do what only God can do (Gen. 18:14; Luke 1:37). God's gift of Himself "cannot be made the symbol of either a new economic system or a new humanity more inclined to make it work."[92] He brings through His redemptive work at Calvary and the empty tomb no mere promise of a coming age, but the new life of that coming age itself (John 3:3, 5). The new creation has begun and it has begun "in Christ" (II Cor. 5:17). "In and through the risen Christ Christian hope is both realistic and realized. The future hope is not a mythic model: it is as real as the bread and fish eaten by the risen Lord. That future hope is also present through the Holy Spirit breathed by the Lord upon His disciples."[93] The kingdom come (Matt. 12:28) is not allegiance to the possible in history. It is the heralding of sins forgiven, the impossible now made actual by the death and physical resurrection of Christ.

It is longing also for the consummation of this beginning in the final ending, the return of Christ in glory. It is the longing of the creation for the day of birth (Rom. 8:19-22). And in between the first taste and the longing, it is the formation of the community of the kingdom for service in the world, "fellow workers for the kingdom of God" (Col. 4:13). "He has made us to be a kingdom" (Rev. 1:6).

The heavenly people of God are called to "walk in a manner worthy of the God who calls . . . into His own kingdom" (I Thess. 2:12). The world in all its dimensions is to taste the "politics" of the kingdom, the pattern, purpose and dynamic by which God orders the life of the heavenly *polis* in this world. It is not the "politics" of this world, for it is a call to "suffer with him" (Rom. 8:18), to put up swords for trowels, and find power in meekness. It is a call to flesh out in the life of the church, the new humanity, the demands of the kingdom, radical, total commitment to Jesus, the bringer of the rule of God.[94]

The church is not to be a retreat where the pious wait for the parousia. Neither is it to be an embarkation point where the armies of the Lord liberate with the sword of Peter (Matt. 26:51-52). There is no continuum between the church as a new nation (I Pet. 2:9) and the world as the history of economic struggle. The poor to whom He preaches the good news are not simply the destitute and oppressed of the world. They are the destitute and oppressed who look to God as the only Liberator (Luke 6:20-26; cf. Ps. 22:27; 25:9; 34:3).[95] "The consolation of Israel" (Luke 2:25) is a baby in the arms of aged Simeon, not a bomb in the hands of a Latin guerrilla. God initiates His program of liberation for the wretched of the earth in the hands of the nail-scarred wretch of Calvary.

Let none of this docetize the realities of history and the realities of our kingdom obligations in history. If the Marxist construct of the kingdom demands much, should less be required of those whose citizenship ultimately is in heaven? To paraphrase the language of Lester DeKoster, until Christians take deeds as well as words into the marketplace, their denunciations of liberation theology will be futile. . . . Until we see in each man a living spirit of "more value than many sparrows," we are not really citizens of the kingdom. "Until we see slums in terms of persons, and not as rents or investments, we are not really citizens of the kingdom. Until we see world hunger in terms of God's opportunity to our charity, and God's demand for an accounting of our stewardship, we cannot feel the fire the kingdom ignites. Until we see factories as associations of persons, not as statistics of production, we cannot see the axe of the kingdom laid to the roots of our trees. Until we earnestly endeavor to bring every economic relation under the dominion of love, we are not effectively demonstrating the realities of the kingdom rule of Christ in our lives."[96]

And should any mission theory or practice docetize the comprehensiveness of the kingdom demands, let it be exorcized. We must question the evangelical tradition that speaks of missionaries as only guests in a country if that tradition does not allow us to call any of Caesar's politics to judgment before the politics of the kingdom of God. We must question the evangelical tradition that re-defines spirituality in such a way that limits our preaching of repentance to the doorkeepers of Herod's palace and not to the Herods. We must question any theorizing of "primary" and "secondary" relationships of the church to the world if that construction allows us to speak for biblical justice only to the left-wing dictatorships of the world and not to the right also.

A third call of liberation theology speaks to the privatization of faith and ecclesiologizing that characterizes the evangelical response to society. It is a call for humanization that seeks to avoid the "pitfalls of 'naiveté' regarding the influences of advanced capitalist society as well as of a narrow ecclesiastical framework."[97] Mirrored in the call of Rubem Alves for "a theology of human hope," it uses the categories popularized by Moltmann but derides the German theologian for providing us with a hope that remains in a future totally beyond our history, hope with a transcendental character not related to any specific situation.[98] Political humanism is to provide the critique capable of transforming the present into a more humanized future. Through it, the oppressed people can turn around and claim their freedom to control the future by negation, they can affirm their own creative potential to a truly new future.

With Alves, this must be a "Messianic humanism," differentiated from a "humanistic messianism" which relies solely on its knowledge of the present situation. Humanistic messianism knows no God and therefore ultimately either despairs of the present and gives up or resorts to hope based on ideals outside history and the historical praxis. Messianic humanism, on the contrary, unleashes a process of secularization in a continuous dynamic process which cannot be bound by law to the status quo. It must never proceed from any law which functions as an ahistorical standard to imitate. Man must liberate himself from the laws perpetuated by the rich to uphold their structures.[99] Man must liberate himself from a conforming consciousness which seeks an absolute outside history. In this setting, God is the power of human liberation which expresses itself in and through the formative events of the life of the community.[100] He is no "metahistorical principle in which the contradictions of history are transcendentally reconciled."[101]

In this process of humanization the bifurcation between church and world becomes an "outworn phrase that should be replaced by 'Church in the world' or 'Church of the world.' "[102] The history of salvation must become the salvation of history. The medieval model of Latin America's colonial period must be abandoned. With it must go the Augustinian model, Vatican II's revised Thomistic model of a dialoguing servant Church. In its place we put the liberation model, the humanized church.[103]

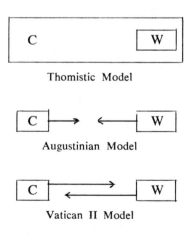

Thomistic Model

Augustinian Model

Vatican II Model

Liberation Model

The church becomes the sacrament-sign community of those who "know" the meaning of humanity and humanity becomes a church "latent." "It is not a matter of first organizing our 'inside' community completely and then going to the world 'outside.' We must be open to the Other outside from the very start."[104]

Liberation-struggle history thus becomes the history of "man becoming." And the mission of the church is no longer one of a "quantitative" notion of saving numbers of souls.[105] Evangelization is to announce the presence of the love of God in the "historical becoming of mankind."[106] Mission has become the celebration of what has been achieved in Christ—human liberation and brotherhood. Mission has become denunciation, the confronting of the present state of social injustice. Mission has become annunciation, the proclamation of the gospel good news "that there is no human act which cannot in the last instance be defined in relation to Christ."[107] The church becomes a sign of the convocation of all men by God. Thus a theology of the Church in the world is refined into "a theology of the world in the Church."[108]

As the evangelical hears this, he cannot be simplistic enough to say that "we should have no quarrel with the goal" defined as "the continuous creation, never ending, of a new way to be a man."[109] Liberation theology's call for man to free and to fulfill himself cannot be isolated from its socio-economic definition of that freedom and applauded as "biblical and right."[110] He must see liberation theology obliterating the distinction between church and world by identifying the purpose of God with the present historical situation. He must see the roots in the anthropocentric vision of man in his historical praxis as the locus of theology. He must see that the end result of such a construction will be that "the Christian becomes, as in the conservative position, a slave to the social order. In spite of all the apparent differences between the revolutionary and the conservative there is basically one essential agreement—both identify the purpose of God with the present historical situation. In the one there is conformity with the *status quo;* in the other a conformity with the revolution."[111]

He must see humanization in such a framework as more than merely the goal of our theorizing but the hermeneutic norm by which our categories of theology are revamped and reinterpreted. Salvation is transformed into economic, political liberation, Christology into love of our neighbor, eschatology into politics, church into humanity, sacraments into human solidarity. It is not enough to say, with Orlando Costas, that "the theology of liberation reveals its *partial* support from the Scripture."[112] It seeks no support from the Scripture in the classic sense. Scripture is historicized from norm to paradigm, from canon to hermeneutic category.[113]

But the evangelical cannot close his ears at this point. He must hear liberation theology asking him other questions. Has the privatized model of evangelical social action leaned too heavily on the notion that society can be changed simply by changing individuals? Does our church-centered view do full justice to the salty role of the people of God in history-shaping? Is there in our ecclesiologizing of the good news of the kingdom an aloofness from the demanding task of social analysis and social change? Does our emphasis on community building run the risk of an introversion of concern? Does the traditional formulation of the "marks of the Church" allow us no continuity with the call to a world task? Does our view of the church in the world close us to an "inside" view of the body of Christ not open to the "outside"?[114]

These questions must call us to a renewed emphasis on the church as God's "new humanity," the community where God in Christ has begun His "new creation" (II Cor. 5:17). He must resist the temptation to compartmentalize the "cultural mandate" (Gen. 1:28) from the "evangelistic mandate" (Matt. 28:18-20), and thus isolate man-in-society from man-in-Christ.[115] He must see the command to the first Adam to be "fruitful and multiply and fill the earth and subdue it; and rule" finding its intiating fulfillment in Christ the second

Adam, who has "all things in subjection under his feet" (Ps. 8:6; Heb. 2:5-8), Himself "the fulness" (Eph. 4:13). And with that, he must see the people of Christ as the "new Adam" (Eph. 2:13-16; 4:13; 4:22-24), empowered now because of the redemptive sovereignty and dominion of Christ earned through His death and resurrection (Matt. 28:18; Acts 2:36; Phil. 2:5-11), called, in the language of Genesis 1:28, to be "the fulness of him who fills all in all" (Eph. 1:23). He must see the church "filled up to all the fulness of God" (Eph. 3:19) and empowered as the beginning of the new humanity to extend the Edenic rule of the second Adam to the ends of the earth, "that he might fill all things" (Eph. 4:8-10).

As the new humanity, he must see the church, renewed after the image of Him who created him (Col. 3:10; Eph. 4:24), as the beginning point of the world's new history, "being transformed into the same image from glory to glory" (II Cor. 3:18). He cannot see the old world as the church but he must see the church as the beginning of the new world. And he must see that new image of God unveiled in the church reflecting in its lifestyle in the world the kingdom patterns of God's original design for the world. He must see in the practice of the new humanity in the world the "putting on of the new man" (Eph. 4:24). The call of God for integrity in the world (Eph. 4:25) that judges with truth and judgment for peace in your gates (Zech. 8:16), the call of God for anger (Eph. 4:26) "at what is worthless and . . . deception" (Ps. 4:2), for the offering of "sacrifices of righteousness and trust in the Lord" (Ps. 4:4), the call of God for "performing with his own hands what is good" (Eph. 4:28) must be expressed in the life of the Adamic community before the world. The word of the people of God before the world must be "good for edification . . . that it may give grace to those who hear" (Eph. 4:29).

This is no call either to status quo or to revolution but to reformation of the status quo and to theocratizing the revolution. It is a God-centered denial of the sacralization of the world and of the secularization of the church. The task of the new humanity of God proceeds in an awareness that the world cannot make the salt of the gospel into the concrete of the secular city and the church remnant cannot become the silent majority of the world. The eschatological dimensions of the Christian hope are always a pilgrim hope, "looking for the city which has foundations, whose architect and builder is God" (Heb. 11:10).

This eschatological perspective is not "escapism" but "realism." It is a call to ministry in the world, to challenge the high places, to "struggle . . . against the rulers, against the powers, against the world forces of this darkness, against the spiritual forces of wickedness in the heavenly places" (Eph. 6:12). "Since all these things are to be destroyed in this way, what sort of people ought you to be in holy conduct and godliness . . ." (II Pet. 3:11)?

Any perspective on this calling, which either reduces its God-centered dynamic to the dimension of liberation theology's "man becoming" or evangelical theology's "churchism," must be exorcized. Any theorizing which reduces its cosmic task by submerging either the church in the world or the world in the church must be exorcized. The mission of the church "will not be Christian simply because, viewed against the background of an apostate philosophy, it is truly *action;* action will be Christian and will be truly action because it is *pro rege*—for the king."[116]

Notes

1. Hugo Assmann, "Basic Aspects of Theological Reflection in Latin America: A Critical Evaluation of the 'Theology of Liberation,'" *Risk* 9, 2 (1973), 28.
2. As Freire uses the term it is a synonym for politicization, awakening the conscience of the dispossessed living in the "culture of silence" to an awareness of their economic, social, and political domination. Cf. Ismael E. Amaya, "The Present Status of the Theology of Revolution in Latin America," *Latin America Pulse* VIII, 1 (January, 1973), 6. We are using the term in a much broader sense.
3. José Miguez-Bonino, *Doing Theology in a Revolutionary Situation* (Philadelphia: Fortress Books, 1975), pp. 38-60.
4. Stephen C. Knapp, p. 10 above.
5. Rudolf Obermüller, *Evangelism in Latin America* (London: Lutterworth Press, 1957), p. 25.

6. Roger Greenway, *An Urban Strategy for Latin America* (Grand Rapids: Baker Book House, 1973), p. 116.
7. *Ibid.*, pp. 116-117.
8. William L. Wonderly and Jorge Lara-Braud, *¿Los Evangélicos Somos Asi?* (Mexico, D. F.: Casa Unida des Publicaciones, S. A., 1964), quoted in *ibid.*, p. 117.
9. Charles Denton, "Latin America in Transition: Social Implications for the Missionary," *World Vision* (March, 1970), 11.
10. René Padilla, "A Steep Climb Ahead for Theology in Latin America," *Evangelical Missions Quarterly* 7, 2 (Winter, 1971), 101.
11. René Padilla, "Theology in Latin America," *Theological News Monograph No. 5* (October, 1972), 2.
12. René Padilla, "The Church and Political Ambiguity," *Christianity Today* XVIII, 21 (July 26, 1974), 41-42.
13. F. Ross Kinsler, "Extension: An Alternative Model for Theological Education," *Learning in Context* (Bromley, Kent: Theological Education Fund, 1973), p. 41.
14. *Ibid.*, pp. 141, 145.
15. W. R. Reid, Victor Monterroso, Harmon Johnson, *Latin American Church Growth* (Grand Rapids: William B. Eerdmans Publishing Co., 1969), p. 295. The authors may exemplify the very point we are making. They preface their remarks by the conditional, "In many cases."
16. Harold Lindsell, "Faith Missions Since 1938," *Frontiers of the Christian World Mission Since 1938,* Wilbur C. Harr, ed. (New York: Harper and Brothers, 1962), pp. 202-208. Lindsell's essay defines "faith missions" largely in terms of those institutions fundamentalist in theology with distinct patterns of personnel and financial support theoretically non-denominational or interdenominational in character. What needs critical analysis are the theological roots of fundamentalism.
17. Charles H. Troutman, "Evangelicals and the Middle Class in Latin America," *Evangelical Missions Quarterly* 7, 2 (Winter, 1971), 86-87.
18. Samuel Escobar, "Urbana '70," *Evangelical Missions Quarterly* 7, 3 (Spring, 1971), 153.
19. Samuel Escobar, "The Social Responsibility of the Church in Latin America," *Evangelical Missions Quarterly* 6, 3 (Spring, 1970), 136-138.
20. Carl F. H. Henry, *Evangelical Responsibility in Contemporary Theology* (Grand Rapids: William B. Eerdmans Publishing Co., 1957), pp. 32-47.
21. Samuel Escobar, "Evangelism and Man's Search for Freedom, Justice and Fulfillment," *Let the Earth Hear His Voice,* J. D. Douglas, ed. (Minneapolis: World Wide Publications, 1975), p. 310.
22. C. Peter Wagner, *Latin American Theology: Radical or Evangelical?* (Grand Rapids: William B. Eerdmans Publishing Co., 1970), p. 15.
23. *Ibid.*, pp. 14-15.

24. A helpful discussion of that concept as it is used in conciliar circles is found in: Donald McGavran, ed., *Eye of the Storm* (Waco, Texas: Word Books, 1972), pp. 205-218; Leighton Ford, "Presence Vs. Proclamation," *Evangelical Missions Quarterly* 4, 4 (Summer, 1968), 204-210.
25. Brian Griffiths, ed., *Is Revolution Change?* (Downers Grove: Inter-Varsity Press, 1972), p. 85.
26. *Ibid.*, p. 92.
27. Harold Lindsell, "The Evangelical Missions: The Home Base," *The Future of the Christian World Mission*, William J. Danker and Wi Jo Kang, eds. (Grand Rapids: William B. Eerdmans Publishing Co., 1971), p. 90.
28. Donald McGavran, ed., *Crucial Issues in Missions Tomorrow* (Chicago: Moody Press, 1972), pp. 9-10.
29. McGavran's emphasis on numbers has been strongly criticized by Padilla in the past, though usually not by name. Cf. René Padilla, "Evangelism and the World," *Let the Earth Hear His Voice*, pp. 125-126, 138-139. There seems some misunderstanding on Padilla's part of the meaning of McGavran's arguments, as he contends it is based on a dualism of quantity and quality. That may be an effect of the argument, but it is not what McGavran himself intends. The source of Padilla's concern may lie more in McGavran's insistence on a distinction between discipling and perfecting.
30. Lewis Smedes, *All Things Made New* (Grand Rapids: William B. Eerdmans Publishing Co., 1970), pp. 92ff.
31. Harvie M. Conn, "How Can I Be Spiritual and at the Same Time Human?," *The Other Side* 9, 5 (September–October, 1973), 16-19, 42-47.
32. Pablo Perez, "Biblical Theology and Cultural Identity in Latin America," *Let the Earth Hear His Voice*, p. 1252.
33. Wagner, *op. cit.*, p. 14.
34. Escobar, *op. cit.*, p. 308.
35. *Ibid.*, p. 316.
36. Wagner, *op. cit.*, pp. 103-109.
37. Rene Padilla, "A Steep Climb Ahead for Theology in Latin America," Evangelical Missions Quarterly 7, 2 (Winter, 1971), 105. The entire essay is a careful treatment of the argument of Wagner's book.
38. Lindsell, *op. cit.*, p. 90.
39. *Let the Earth Hear His Voice*, pp. 4-5. John R. W. Stott, a key framer of the Covenant, reflects this duality further in his analysis in *Christian Mission in the Modern World* (Downers Grove: Inter-Varsity Press, 1975), pp. 26-27.
40. Christian Lalive d'Epinay, *Haven of the Masses* (London: Lutterworth Press, 1969), p. 145.
41. Emilio Willems, *Followers of the New Faith* (Nashville: Vanderbilt

University Press, 1967); Greenway, *op. cit.,* pp. 119-120; Peter Wagner, *Look Out! The Pentecostals Are Coming* (Carol Stream: Creation House, 1973), pp. 137-148.

42. Eugene Nida, *Understanding Latin Americans* (South Pasadena: William Carey Library, 1974), pp. 22-26.

43. Peter Savage, Jose María Blanch, Charles F. Denton, *Protestant Belief Systems in Three Latin American Countries: A Preliminary Survey* (Cochabamba, Bolivia: Board of Communication 'Rex Mundi,' n.d.), p. 10.

44. *Ibid.,* p. 11

45. C. Peter Wagner, *Frontiers in Missionary Strategy* (Chicago: Moody Press, 1971), p. 207.

46. Wagner, *Look Out! The Pentecostals Are Coming,* p. 139.

47. Wagner, *Latin American Theology: Radical or Evangelical?,* p. 104.

48. Escobar, *op. cit.,* p. 325.

49. Perez, *op. cit.,* p. 1256.

50. Gustavo Gutiérrez, *A Theology of Liberation* (Maryknoll: Orbis books, 1973), p. 15.

51. Rosemary Reuther, *Liberation Theology* (New York: Paulist Press, 1972), p. 176. The comment is not altogether clear but is likely an effort to differentiate the methodology of liberation theology from the cognitively oriented theologies of the North Atlantic. The statement's weakness is its failure to perceive the theology of liberation as an *a priori* fully as dogmatic as any preceding it.

52. A. Schaff, *Filosofía del Hombre: ¿Marx or Sartre?* (Mexico, 1965), pp. 109, 118-120, quoted in: Andrew Kirk, "The Meaning of Man in the Debate Between Christianity and Marxism," *Theological Fraternity Bulletin,* 2 (1974), 5.

53. Robert D. Knudsen, "Anathema or Dialogue?," *Westminster Theological Journal* XXXIV, 2 (May, 1972), 147-148.

54. Kirk, *loc. cit.* For a general discussion of Marxism, see J. van der Hoeven, *et al., Marxisme en Revolutie* (Amsterdam: Buijten en Schipperheijn, 1967), pp. 11ff.

55. Gutierrez, *op. cit.,* p. 79.

56. *Ibid.,* p. 11.

57. Hugo Assmann, *Practical Theology of Liberation* (London: Search Press, Ltd., 1975), pp. 82-83.

58. Hugo Assmann, *Opresión-Liberación: Deasfío a los cristianos* (Montivideo: Tierra Nueva, 1971), pp. 13-14.

59. *Ibid.,* p. 116.

60. *Ibid.,* p. 117.

61. James F. Conway, *Marx and Jesus: Liberation Theology in Latin America* (New York: Carlton Press, Inc., 1973), p. 94; Gutiérrez, *op.*

cit., pp. 220-225; Assmann, *Practical Theology of Liberation,* pp. 80-81, 84.

62. Assmann, *op. cit.,* p. 59.
63. *Ibid.,* p. 104.
64. René de Visme Williamson, in his essay, "The Theology of Liberation," *Christianity Today* XIX, 22 (Aug. 8, 1975), 7-13, reacts in the most general of ways. Even the written reflections of Padilla and Escobar cited thus far fail largely to interact at this point.
65. The excellent chapter in this collection by Knapp draws attention to the importance of praxis as a limiting concept in the construction but does not interact with it because of the author's admitted lack of study in "Marxism, capitalism or just plain reality enough to know the extent to which the class struggle hypothesis holds up under 'biased-for the poor' scrutiny" (p. 23). This is a far cry from the presuppositions of Peter Wagner, who evaluates the movement in terms of McGavran's church growth concepts (*op. cit.,* pp. 67-74). Orlando Costas, a radical evangelical, similarly reduces it largely to a sociological conflict between functionalist and structuralist approaches. Cf. *The Church and Its Mission: A Shattering Critique from the Third World* (Wheaton: Tyndale House, 1974), pp. 225-227.
66. Miguez-Bonino, *op. cit.,* pp. 95-96.
67. Knapp, *op. cit.,* p. 18.
68. S. U. Zuidema, *Communication and Confrontation* (Toronto: Wedge Publishing Foundation, 1972), p. 121.
69. *Ibid.,* p. 122.
70. L. Kalsbeck, *Contours of a Christian Philosophy* (Toronto: Wedge Publishing Foundation, 1975), p. 349; Herman Dooyeweerd, *A New Critique of Theoretical Thought* (Philadelphia: Presbyterian and Reformed Publishing Co., 1955), II, 293.
71. John M. Frame, *Van Til: The Theologian* (Phillipsburg, N. J.: Pilgrim Publishing Co., 1976), p. 25.
72. Assmann, *op. cit.,* p. 76.
73. Frame, *loc cit.*
74. Assmann, *op. cit.,* p. 80.
75. Costas, *op. cit.,* p. 252.
76. *Loc cit.*
77. Gutiérrez, *op. cit.,* pp. 168-169.
78. *Ibid.,* p. 236.
79. *Ibid.,* p. 238.
80. *Ibid.,* p. 217ff.
81. Assmann, *Opresión-Liberación: Deasfío a los cristianos,* p. 80.
82. Gutiérrez, *op. cit.,* p. 218.
83. *Ibid.,* p. 15.
84. Miguez-Bonino, *op. cit.,* p. 152.
85. *Ibid.,* p. 138.

86. *Ibid.*, p. 133.
87. *Ibid.*, p. 136.
88. *Ibid.*, p. 143.
89. Assmann, *Practical Theology of Liberation,* pp. 34-35.
90. *Ibid.*, p. 35.
91. Edmund P. Clowney, "The Politics of the Kingdom" (unpublished paper, Westminster Theological Seminary, Philadelphia, 1975), 4.
92. *Ibid.*, 7.
93. *Ibid.*, 14.
94. Herman Ridderbos, *The Coming of the Kingdom* (Philadelphia: Presbyterian and Reformed Publishing Co., 1962), pp. 322-329.
95. *Ibid.*, pp. 185-192.
96. Lester DeKoster, *Communism and Christian Faith* (Grand Rapids: William B. Eerdmans Publishing Co., 1956), p. 118.
97. Gutiérrez, *op. cit.*, p. 225.
98. Rubem Alves, *A Theology of Human Hope* (Washington, D. C.: Corpus Books, 1969), pp. 55-63.
99. *Ibid.*, p. 110.
100. *Ibid.*, p. 90.
101. *Ibid.*, p. 91.
102. Assmann, *op. cit.*, p. 65.
103. Sidney Rooy, "The Challenge to Reformed Higher Education in the Latin Third World Countries" (paper presented at the University of Potchefstroom Conference on Reformed Higher Education, 1975), 7-8.
104. Enrique Dussel, *History and the Theology of Liberation* (Maryknoll: Orbis Books, 1976), p. 154.
105. Gutierrez, *op. cit.*, p. 150.
106. *Ibid.*, p. 205.
107. *Ibid.*, p. 268.
108. *Ibid.*, p. 261.
109. John R. W. Stott, *op. cit.*, p. 93, commends the goal in exactly this language.
110. *Loc. cit.*
111. Griffiths, *op. cit.*, p. 82.
112. Costas, *op. cit.*, p. 258.
113. Harvie M. Conn, *Teologia Contemporanea en el Mundo* (Grand Rapids: Subcomisión Literatura Cristiana de la Iglesia Christiana Reformada, 1975), pp. 86-87.
114. Knapp, *op. cit.*, p. 33.
115. Arthur Glasser seems to suggest this compartmentalization in his formulation of the question. See "The Evangelicals: World Outreach," *The Future of the Christian World Mission,* p. 110.
116. Knudsen, *op. cit.*, 151.

5. Contextualization: Where Do We Begin?

HARVIE M. CONN

At the heart of the theology of liberation is the affirmation of "the contextual nature of theology."[1] Deliberately so, it begins "by appropriating the historical process of the oppressed classes' struggle for emancipation in Latin America," recognizing as it does that "refusal to indulge in abstract theologizing is in itself, however, no assurance of contextuality."[2] It calls for more, for "an unambiguous political commitment" to reality appropriated in what it calls "its historical concreteness." So, in 1971, José Miguez-Bonino raised the question, "What does theology speak about?" and answers it by affirming theology's self-reflection on "that concrete reality in which we find ourselves," the missiological challenge which "that concrete reality presents to Christians in that continent."[3] This concrete rootedness is a liberation theology's call for contextualization, for a theology "which does not stop with reflecting on the world, but rather tries to be part of the process through which the world is transformed. It is a theology which is open—in the protest against trampled human dignity, in the struggle against the plunder of the vast majority of people, in liberating love, and in the building of a new, just and fraternal society—to the gift of the Kingdom of God."[4] In its understanding of contextualization is its self-understanding "as a *new way* to do theology."

What are the parameters of contextualization and the debate which surrounds it? What part has the theology of liberation played in the formation of the debate? How shall we begin the erection of evangelical guidelines that respond in constructive dialogue to liberation theology's questions in the contextualization debate?

The Debate

In 1972, the Theological Education Fund of the World Council of Churches published *Ministry in Context,* presenting the third mandate program (1970–1977) of its work to the churches. Reflecting a conscious change of emphasis from the call for "Advance" of the first mandate's post-colonial era (1958–1964) and the call for "Rethink" in the second mandate (1965–1969),[5] the focus turned to "Reform" and more specifically "contextuality" and "contextualization" as the way towards reform in theological education.

The seeds of this last shift, however, had been present from the start. Even in the first stage, when the focus "showed a deep concern for better trained and better educated ministry" defined in terms of "the raising of the level of scholarship and striving for academic excellence,"[6] a supplementary statement that the TEF should seek "to develop and strengthen indigenous theological education" was reinforcing a growing uneasiness about "whether the pursuit of Western standards would necessarily strengthen indigenous theological education."[7] This concern became more explicit in the second mandate period as the younger churches more self-consciously rejected the colonial image of themselves as the object of missions and became the subject in missions. As participants "in the *Missio Dei* in and for the world,"[8] a new missiological thrust surfaced in their definition of the excellence to be sought in theological education. It was to be defined "in terms of that kind of theological training which leads to a real encounter between the student and the Gospel in terms of his own forms of thought and culture, and to a living dialogue between the church and its environment. The aim should be to use resources so as to help teachers and students to a deeper understanding of the Gospel in the context of the particular cultural and religious setting of the church. . . ."[9] The culmination of this process of historical development was the growing conviction "that theological education, for better or for worse, occurs invariably as interaction between text and context, and out of this interaction the form is shaped."[10] Those convictions were embodied in the introduction of the term, "contextualization," and its specific understanding within the conciliar movement.

From Indigenization to Contextualization

The roots of the contextualization debate lie deeper than some

91

recognize[11] in the growing ecumenical frustrations over the nineteenth-century formulations of the "indigenous church." Structured by mission theorists like Henry Venn and Rufus Anderson,[12] the formulation was conceived to guarantee the native church planted by the missionary its proper dignity as a people of God. This it sought to achieve by defining the mission church as self-supporting, self-governing, and self-propagating. Born in the colonial era of missions, its stated aim was commitment to the establishment of "a genuinely native church,"[13] freed from missionary domination.

In the years following World War II, discussions within the International Missionary Council emphasized the weaknesses of the formulation, particularly in terms of its inadequacies for expressing the "full spiritual equality" of the world church in a "common calling," as "partners in obedience." Between the Whitby Conference of 1947 and the Willingen Conference of 1952, the accent of frustration shifted from one over church-mission relations to one over the nature of mission itself. Under the impact of the Willingen theme of the *World Mission of the Church*, indigenous became indigenization. The three-self formula was seen to "have meaning only as expressions of the church's worshipping and witnessing character. We need to apply tests deeper in content and wider in scope. These should follow from the church's nature as a worshipping, witnessing and expectant body."[14] Drawn now in a context of mission rather than missions, indigenization, as the expression of "the universal church in its local setting," was to be seen in four marks: (1) Relatedness to the soil—ability to make elements of local cultures captive to Christ, (2) possession of an adequately trained ministry, a ministry adapted to local requirements, (3) an inner spiritual life, nurturing the Christian community, witnessing to the unevangelized, and (4) membership in the church universal.

At this stage of the debate, elements of continuity with past formulations could be seen in the call for "an adequately trained ministry" and in the need for evangelism. But a new thrust can also be seen in the relation of indigenization as a concept to cultural relatedness, "a ministry adapted to local requirements." These elements were to provide the line of continuity with the current call for "contextualization," and a refinement of what that cultural relatedness demanded in terms of the nature of the gospel itself. "So," says Coe, "in using the word *contextualization,* we try to convey all that is implied in the familiar term indigenization, yet seek to press beyond for a more dynamic concept which is open to change and which is also future-oriented."[15]

This link with conciliar discussions in the past becomes even more apparent in the theological concept of *Missio Dei* and history as the hermeneutic of God's speaking in the world, with which it is associated in the TEF discussion. Coe comments, "Contextuality . . . is that critical assessment of what makes the context really significant in the light of the *Missio Dei.* It is the missiological discernment of the signs of the times, seeing where God is at work and calling us to participate in it."[16] It takes place at that point "where the Church, whether in the global or local sense, 'walks on the water' in faith, heeding the signs which are God's way of talking to us in our time and context. Relevance takes contextuality seriously by discerning God's mission for man in history. . . ."[17] The definition builds on the formulations of Uppsala 1968 and its structuring of mission which transformed the history of salvation into the salvation of history and removes the line between the church and the world.[18] In this restructuring, the world, not the church, becomes the central focus of God's redeeming activity, a "salvation today" understood as humanization in the general historical process.[19]

Flowing from this hermeneutical elevation of history are those distinctives that isolate contextualization from its past in indigeneity, reinforcing the new dimensions of its emphasis. On the simplest level, there is a difference in situation. "Indigenization tends to be used in the sense of responding to the Gospel in terms of a traditional culture. Contextualization, while not ignoring this, takes into account the process of secularity, technology and the struggle for human justice, which characterizes the historical moment of nations in the Third World."[20] Indigenization was a formula written against "patterns of dependence typical of the colonial period," whereas contextualization speaks to "the more radically politicized situations in Asia, Africa, and Latin America" forcing "the issue of whether the national churches and theological colleges can develop more authentic, contextualized patterns as expressions of missiological faithfulness."[21]

In this milieu, contextualization is to be constructed, unlike the old formulae, on what has been wisely termed "the dialectic of the text and context—the situational character of all theology."[22] Contextualization is a dialectical process of "involvement and participation, out of which critical awareness may arise."[23] It is more than simply taking all contexts seriously. It is the "conscientization of the contexts in the particular, historical moment, assessing the peculiarity of the context in the light of the mission of the church as it is called to participate in the *Missio Dei*."[24] Only through the dialectical interaction of the *Missio Dei* and the historical process does the gospel's contextualization take concrete shape. "Authentic contextualization is always prophetic, arising always out of a genuine encounter between God's Word and His world, and moves toward the purpose of challenging and changing the situation through rootedness in and commitment to a given historical moment."[25]

In this dialectical process, one should not be deceived by references to "God's Word" and "the text" into identifying these terms with the Bible. Coe, in commenting on the third mandate, makes a sharp distinction between "the Text which transcends all, because it is directed to and derived from the transcendent reality of God in Christ" and "interpreted texts" as "mere earthen vessels," having "to be reformed and reinterpreted."[26] The texts are merely derivative pointers to the Text. Thus, the "Church's task will always be to so invade the historical context of the biblical text and to so grasp the present context of God's redemptive activity in Christ, that the text becomes again appropriately contextualized and the Gospel heard and responded to. We cannot simply assume that we know what the Gospel was there and then any more than we can simply assume that we know what it is here and now."[27] As Knapp writes, "in this construction, the once-and-for-all, the 'given' component of the Gospel is a transcendent reality that comes to expression in various human forms 'texts') which is the result of a 'double wrestle' with the transcendent Text and the situation."[28]

94

From Contextualization to Liberation

Liberation theology doubtless could be comfortable with the TEF's call for a dialectic of text and context in which history yields the praxis of the situation. José Miguez-Bonino notes that "when Assmann speaks of the rejection of 'any *logos* which is not the *logos* of a *praxis*' or Gutiérrez writes about an 'epistemological split,' they are not merely saying that truth must be applied, or even that truth is related to its application. They are saying, in fact, that there is no truth outside or beyond the concrete historical events in which men are involved as agents. There is, therefore, no knowledge except in action itself, in the process of transforming the world through participation in history."[29]

In another area also, the melting of contextualization and liberation theology can easily be supposed. It is what Knapp refers to as contextualization's "epistemological revolution"—theology as participation.[30] Not that manifest in the official TEF documents, it is nevertheless implicit enough for Aharon Sapsezian, one of the Fund's directors, to seek to make it explicit in his analysis. It would seem to flow from the dialectical interaction of the *Missio Dei* and the historical process. Repeated affirmations of contextualization as "a dynamic not a static process,"[31] "the issues of social justice and human development" as demanding gospel expression and response, "the determinant goal of its work,"[32] make it easy to see why Sapsezian can blend contextualization's call for participation, involvement within one's context with liberation theology's call for concreteness. Contextualization's solidarity with change in history is seen as not far from liberation theology's methodological principle of praxis as "action which believes in the possibilities of changing oppressive human institutions."[33] Contextualization's dialectic tension between doing theology and transforming the world seems easily to flow into Paulo Freire's warnings concerning "verbalism" and "activism." "Within the word we find two dimensions, reflection and action, in such a radical interaction that if one is sacrificed—even in part—the other immediately suffers. There is no true word that is not at the same time a praxis. Thus, to speak a true word is to transform the world."[34]

Contextualization's argument that "authentic theological reflection can take place only as the *theologia in loco,* discerning the contextuality within the concrete context,"[35] is not a far cry from Assmann's fear of some "primary source of 'truth in itself.' "[36] Contextualization calls for "the conscientization of the contexts in the particular, historical moment. . . . Such conscientization can only come through involvement and participation, out of which critical awareness may arise."[37] Liberation theology calls for a conscientization that learns "to perceive social, political and economic contradictions and to take action against the oppressive elements of reality."[38]

But, in spite of these areas of continuity between contextualization and liberation theology, one needs also to do some justice to their discontinuity.[39] They are reflected most strongly in the response of Victor Nazario to the issues discussed in the Third Mandate Programme of the TEF. Nazario's skepticism is not over the intrinsic nature of contextualization, with which he basically agrees, but on the "weakness of the principles which lead to it."[40] He focuses specifically on the three main concerns which serve in the original report as point of departure for the understanding of contextuality, and reinforces, as he does, liberation theology's concern for even a contextualized abstraction from the realities of history. So, for example, in his treatment of the Mandate's call for a gospel response "to the issues of social justice and human development," he sees these two issues as self-induced wishes, "highly influenced by the thrust of industrialism and technocracy," and therefore more symptomatic of "the oppressive forces of neo-colonialism which present themselves under the guise of social justice and human development."[41] He calls instead for "indigenous awareness," "the process by which inherent and inherited values are brought into conscious awareness."[42] In the same vein, he repudiates the Third Mandate call for an awareness to the dialectic involved between the cultures and religions of the Third World and a universal technological civilization. "Technology," he says, "is a western product used by the western world for the benefit of the western world. We cannot speak of any technology (as referred to in the programme) that is not part of the technocratic bureaucracy which constitutes the technological monopoly of the west."[43] Behind all this he sees lurking again the division of the world into two hemispheres: the producers and the consumers.

In all of this, Nazario is repeating liberation theology's attack on developmentalism as escape from radical change.[44] But beyond that, he is reminding us that contextualization's methodology, insofar as it is not radical in its application of praxis to history, is also a form of docetic flight from reality. Liberation theology refuses any idealist approach, even one as cordial as contextualization, if all it does is seek to "understand" culture rather than discover and liberate it. The contextualization demanded by liberation theology cannot become a "fad" or a "catchword" by abstraction from the economic dialectic of history. The political dimensions of liberation theology's understanding of history and the Marxist standards by which it analyzes those dimensions do not seem as operative in the more general references of the TEF Programme.

Evangelical Response to the Debate

Evangelicalism's voice has been slow being heard in the contextualization discussion. One of the first places where it seemed to surface with visibility was the Lausanne International Congress on World Evangelization. An address by Dr. Byang H. Kato and a study group on "The Gospel, Contextualization and Syncretism" opened up some of the parameters of the discussion.[45] The focus of Kato's address concentrated on the transmission of the gospel in ways relevant to the receptor culture, and warned of the dangers of syncretism in such a process. And, in many ways, his treatment may be reflective of evangelical thinness of treatment. Abstracting the message of the gospel from its form, Kato's argument concentrates largely on the expressions of the culture in worship—liturgy, dress, ecclesiastical services. It seems to take little cognizance of the shift from indigenization to contextualization, and especially to the heart of the contextualization debate—the gospel in interaction with the culture. At the linguistic level, where it comes closest to the debate, he concedes only that the "terminology of theology should be expressed the way common people can understand."[46] But even

97

there, he is fearful of dynamic equivalence translations. "Instead of employing terms that would water down the Gospel, the congregations should be taught the meaning of the term as originally meant. One instance is the mustard seed. . . . Instead of substituting it with a local grain, the term should be employed and the explanation given."[47] There is no interaction with the contextualization debate except in his treatment of African natural theology advocates like Mbiti and Idowu. And again, the reaction is completely negative. There is no admission in Kato's address (though more in the report of the study group) of the enculturation process which has often marked even the evangelical proclamation of the gospel in Third World contexts. The Lausanne Covenant does better, acknowledging that "missions have all too frequently exported with the Gospel an alien culture, and churches have sometimes been in bondage to culture rather than to Scripture."[48]

A great part of the quietude within evangelical circles on the question may flow from the isolation of missions from theology and theological reflection that often seems characteristic of North America. Samuel Escobar commented recently on such feelings that surfaced during the preparation phases of the Congress. "Lausanne should be a 'how to do it' Congress, was their argument. . . ."[49] This was aggravated following the Congress, he continues, "by the conservative backlash . . . for which Pasadena was partly responsible. . . . The answer from Pasadena, that expressed also the feelings of others, was: 'There is nothing to redefine. We have already heard the voice long ago and that is written and packaged. Let us carry on business as usual but in a far greater scale.' "[50] North American cultural pragmatism, coupled with a legitimate fear of liberal constructions, can easily serve to cripple a full discussion of the dimensions of the problem of hermeneutic, raised again by a growing evangelical awareness of the point of contact between the gospel and the dynamic of the world's alien cultures.

And even more frightening is the possible repetition of such quiescent neglect in the Latin American church, where the theology of liberation is the most vocal, though still a minority, proponent of contextualization. René Padilla speaks tirelessly of that church

98

as "a church without theology,"[51] dependent for its theology on North America, manifesting the same divorce between evangelism and theology, the gospel lacking contextualization in its culture. With endorsement he quotes the frightening words of José Miguez-Bonino, "Neither Roman Catholicism nor Protestantism, as churches, has rooted deeply enough in Latin American human reality to produce creative thinking. In other words, both churches have remained on the fringe of the history of our peoples."[52] It is mirrored in the optimistic discounting of such questions by the authors of *Latin American Church Growth*. "European and North American theological emphases concerning secularized Christianity find little echo in Latin America, where the Evangelical Church is too busy fulfilling its mission to be troubled by these theological issues."[53] Emilio Antonio Nuñez, director of the Central American Seminary, Guatemala, though far less strident than Padilla, concedes that "it may be said that a serious effort in contextualization is only beginning among us. . . . In Latin America we are far behind in the training of leaders capable of carrying out contextualization: leaders rooted deeply in the Word of God and fully identified with their own culture; leaders who know well the *Text* and the *context*. . . ."[54]

Since Lausanne, a degree of interest has begun to appear in evangelical discussions. One of three group discussions carried on at the 1975 EFMA Mission Executives Retreat concentrated on the question of contextualization after hearing three papers on the topic. Though not official statements of the Retreat, the group's notes echo much of the Lausanne discussion, recognizing a twofold scope to contextualization, "seeking for a correctly applied theology which avoids the dangers of syncretism, and . . . applying it to the current problems of our times. An illustration of the latter would be to determine a theology of liberation as it relates to many Christians in the Third World. . . ."[55] Flowing from an admission that North American missions "are carrying Old World ideas even into the Gospel today," the group concedes, in rather paternalistic language, "that we should permit Third World churches the freedom to express salvation through Christ alone that will bring meaning and life eternal to man in every clime and culture."[56] Again, there is no indication in either

99

the papers or the group report of an outline of the full theological contours of the question as raised by the TEF analysis. And it might be argued the analysis of the question is better fitted to the question of indigenization than contextualization. Consistently the discussion follows the argument of Emilio Antonio Nuñez's paper, isolating the content of the message of the gospel (theology) from the context (culture), but brought together "by means of effective communication."[57] Contextualization and liberation theology depart from indigenization formulae precisely here. They question the equation of the gospel and theology, the meaning of theology implied in this equation, and the isolation of the message from the context in any way. The discussion does not deal sensitively or fully or constructively with any of these questions.

A measure of sophistication is also beginning to appear, but more often from anthropologists than theologians,[58] and then in isolation from the formal dimensions of the contextualization discussion.[59] Within these more advanced forums, the fear often is expressed that the "rather amorphous middle position termed 'evangelicalism,' " living between a left wing capitulation to ethnology-sociology and a right wing reaction to the same disciplines, seems "more ready to expend their time and energy in defense of older formulations of Christian truths than to grapple with the matter of reformulating these truths in terms of new conceptual frameworks."[60] Awareness of gospel-cultural interaction "has led them to embrace and develop a supposedly presuppositionless 'Biblical Theology' (as opposed to philosophical or systematic theology). This . . . approach to a solution has, however, all too often simply reduced the awareness of the theologians (and of their students) to the philosophic nature of their conceptual framework."[61] The author would also add the alternative fear, seldom expressed by the evangelical anthropologist but often illustrated by him,[62] that the growing interest in what some have labelled ethnotheology or "contextual theology"[63] (as opposed to systematic theology) may be done without sufficient attention to a biblically critical analysis of the systems of anthropology and sociology and appropriated by the evangelical and, in their haste for a pragmatically applied missionary anthropology, lead us again into a capitulation to humanistic patterns overlaid on the Scripture. Not only must Christian truth be reformulated in terms of new conceptual frameworks. The conceptual frameworks themselves must be reformulated in terms of the Scripture.[64] Presuppositionlessness is an impossibility in either "Biblical Theology" or anthropology.[65]

The most useful contribution to an evaluation of contextualization thus far seems to have come from Steven Knapp's as yet unpublished paper on "Contextualization and Its Implications for U.S. Evangelical Churches and Missions." Knapp's criticisms of the TEF documents and the theology of liberation as an exposition of that concept of contextualization focuses on three areas of concern, the views of revelation, ecclesiology, and missiology underlying the structure. But all of these he sees as flowing from "a fundamental, underlying structure in which all of the elements are integrated."[66] That integrating structure, we would suggest, is the operative of a hermeneutic of history in place of the hermeneutic of Scripture.

The primacy of that historical hermeneutic is captured in the words of the 1972 TEF report and its understanding of the *Missio Dei* as "heeding the signs which are God's way of talking to us in our time and context. Relevance takes contextuality seriously by discerning God's mission for man in history."[67] What is called "the incarnational nature of the Word" must seek to take into account that which characterizes "the historical moment of nations in the Third World."[68] Liberation theology re-echoes that primacy of historical hermeneutic by reminding us that "God builds his Kingdom from and within human history in its entirety; his action is a constant call and challenge to man. . . . History, in relation to the Kingdom, is not a riddle to be solved but a mission to be fulfilled,"[69] a concentration of "true history" in real history. Says Gutiérrez, "theological discourse . . . is about a word that is located in the midst of history."[70] Unlike contextualization, however, it is not content with defining that "historical moment of nations" simply in terms of "the process of secularity, technology and the struggle for human justice."[71] Secularity for the liberation theologian is not a "crisis of Faith" in the Third World as in the Western World. It is a full partner in a "dialogical situation" where faith is more often "seen as privilege which is conditioned by geographical and sociological conditions."[72] Technology is not a universal category of history but "a western product used by the western world for the benefit of the western world," a monopoly "which has divided the world into two hemispheres: the producers and the consumers."[73] Thus, for liberation theology, the struggle for human justice is not one with the process of secularity and technology. Its very meaning is defined in its struggle against secularity and technology.

The fruits of such a hermeneutic undermine "the necessity of an authoritative *interpretation* to adequately discern revelatory events, and the unique place of the apostolic witness to Christ as a guide for discernment of both the work of Christ in the past and his ongoing work in contemporary history. And does the tendency to reduce revelation to salvation, word to event do justice, in the end, to the importance of language?"[74] Given such a hermeneutic of history as action-reflection, how can Scripture function as the *norm* in theology, understood in a more traditional sense, or even in the liberation theology sense of discernment of one's context? Even granting, as we must, the culturally conditioned perspectives of our exegesis, can contextual or liberation theology do justice to the received tradition of the gospel that has been properly the evangelical concern behind "systematic" theology?[75]

The same frustrations occur as the hermeneutic demands a new view of ecclesiology and missiology, the church as "the sacrament of history," the visible, universal sign "of the presence of the Lord within the aspiration for liberation and the struggle for a more human and just society."[76] The church's identity becomes defined in terms of its participation in this hermeneutic event of history, participation in the general historical process, and more particularly in its liberating and humanizing process. There is what Knapp calls "a corresponding diminishing of the distinction between the church and the world and a radical re-interpretation of the mission of the church to and in the world. The understandings associated with the *Missio Dei* concept are undoubtedly at the heart of the issue at this point."[77] The reality of the process of humanization cannot function as the church's hermeneutical base-line.

102

These disagreements function on the level of analysis as well as the level of prescription.[78] Liberation theology's formula for prescription also becomes the analysis by which the situation is defined. At the same time, there are "moments of truth" in the contextualization demands that must be squarely faced and admitted by evangelical missiology. This does not demand the search for a new norm in judging culture. But it does demand that the evangelical cry of *sola Scriptura* be seen as often compromised by the addendum of Western enculturation processes. Too often *Scriptura applicata* has become *Scriptura asarka*. There has been a "failure to grasp enough of the biblical picture, the details of which are a necessary part of the framework, through an unconscious and uncritical absorption of western" cultural patterns.[79] There has been an evangelical failure of awareness of our cultural boundness, and a failure on our part to de-contextualize through a more radical faithfulness to the New Testament. The evangelical practice of hermeneutic remains simply one of the confrontation of "ancient texts" rather than also one of confrontation with present historical reality. Liberation theology calls for a contextualization where the "text" is our situation.[80] But the evangelical response calls for a contextualization in which "the Word of God is reduced to a *logos asarkos* (unincarnate word), a message that touches our lives only on a tangent. The Gospel still has a foreign sound, or no sound at all, in relation to many of the dreams and anxieties, problems and questions, values and customs in the Third World."[81] It has blown that uncertain sound in the north. Why should it be any less uncertain in the south?

Guidelines for an Evangelical Theory of Contextualization

Liberation theology calls us to the conscientization of hermeneutic, a contextualization rooted in the concreteness of history as *Missio Dei*. Evangelical theology in Latin America practices a hermeneutic distant from that concreteness, a conscientization process "which holds that everything that surrounds us is 'worldly' and that since it does not contribute anything to a truly 'spiritual' development. It has to be eliminated radically."[82] Liberation theology equates hermeneutic with the world, evangelical theology with the Word. To the one, the content of the gospel is defined simply in terms of historical praxis, to the other it is defined simply in terms of the written Word of God.[83] Where shall we turn?

An adequate beginning cannot be made by isolating contextualization into a simple category of the effective communication of the content of the gospel to the cultural context.[84] Such a definition does not grasp adequately the challenge offered in the transition of the debate from indigenization to contextualization and freezes the evangelical response to a stage of the controversy that has passed. The response is no doubt seeking to preserve the status of Scripture as subject in the normative process, but it does not do full justice to the other element in any discussion of Scripture as norm, the context in which Scripture norms, human culture, the object of the normative process. Interaction is livelier if we begin by seeing contextualization as the process of the conscientization of the whole people of God to the hermeneutical obligations of the gospel. It must flow from an awareness of the threefold office of the *laos* as prophets, priests, and kings. Contextualization calls all of the body of Christ to the task of theology, to the task of applying Scripture as judge and saviour to the whole texture of our culturally bound lives. A contextual ministry addresses not one, but two, questions to our cultures. How are the divine demands of the gospel of the kingdom communicated in cultural thought forms meaningful to the real issues and needs of the person and his society in that point of cultural time? How shall the man of God, as a member of the body of Christ and the fellowship of the Spirit, respond meaningfully and with integrity to the Scripture so that he may live a full-orbed kingdom lifestyle in covenant obedience with the covenant community?

The program for such a contextualized ministry of the household of faith demands the development of a Christian mind (II Cor. 10: 3-5) that does more than merely baptize the world's agenda or reduce God's agenda to souls instead of the cosmos. It demands we listen carefully to both Scripture and culture, without either acculturating the Bible through allegorizing it into models, or biblicizing our culture through accommodation. It is not content with transforming political, economic, social, and cultural spheres of life until

104

those spheres and their presuppositional framework has been subjected to the judgment of the Word of God. In that sense, the demand for de-contextualization, ignored largely by both liberation theologian and evangelical, becomes as important as contextualization.[85] It does not take up the questions of culture without evaluating the legitimacy of the questions themselves. Neither is it content with the oversimplification that defines the self-understanding of the church either in terms of participation in politicization or in terms of participation in spiritualization. It cannot be content with defining contextualization as a theological process wholly in terms of "critical reflection on the pastoral action of the Church"[86] or in terms of "a spirituality without discipleship in the daily social, economic, and political aspects of life."[87] The one leads to a religionization of the revolution, the other to a Christianization of the status quo. How may the people of God be the fellowship of the Spirit in politics, in economics, in the home, in the bush? How does the *colonia* of the kingdom of God emerge in the *barrios* of Latin America? Calvinism has long asked similar questions. But in the process of "old world" acculturation and translation into the cultural patterns of the "new world" and the "Third World," the cosmic dimensions of the Reformed faith often have been limited to a reductionism better described as conservative-evangelical, leaving the *laos* of God without a sense of world calling or else broadened to an expansionism that leaves the church without a God-centered perspective.

Contextualization, however, cannot be accomplished if it remains simply a program, a theorizing. Ultimately it merges our two questions of proclamation and presence into one, "doing the will of God" (Matt. 6:10; 7:21) in "doing the truth" (I John 1:6). Thus "every command of Christ through the Scripture is de facto a command to contextualize. Whether it is a command to love one's neighbor or to disciple the nations, it has not been obeyed until one has struggled with the necessity of utilizing, rejecting, or transforming cultural forms in the process of response and obedience."[88] In this sense, it calls all Christians to the task of theology, of being involved in the ongoing 'dialectic' between the answers of Scripture and the questions implicit in one's situation.[89] It cannot condemn the Latin

American church as a "church without theology" if it means simply a church with no theoretical reflection of its own.[90] For theoretical abstractions of a theological sort are not theology. But if such a condemnation means by theology the concretization of the Scripture in the possession of the culture for Christ, it speaks truth. Theology as the discipled (not disciplined) reflection/action of "knowing God" is never theology if it is less than functional, carrying out God's plan through His people in His world.

At the heart of the evangelical process of contextualization must be God, the originator, the center and the end of the theopolitical dimensions of the kingdom. He cannot be invested by "projecting" onto Him "the major limitations of Western society,"[91] for He sits on His throne in solitary majesty, jealous of the Baal consorts of Canaan or Wall Street. Neither can His redemptive sovereignty be described as "adequate only when from the history of salvation we pass on to the salvation of history in man."[92] His rule may not be described as "totally other," nor may our experience of that rule be made analogous to Jacob's wrestling with the angel, man wrestling with history in the process of liberation.[93] He may not be reduced by evangelical hypertrophy to an abstraction concerned over the length of women's skirts and the frequency of fiestas nor by liberation hypertrophy in which His sovereignty over men and cultures is de-absolutized into identification with the concrete social reality. He cannot share His glory with history or reduce it by the evangelical process of privatization to the success of an Evangelism-in-Depth campaign. Evangelism-in-Depth must become In-Depth Evangelism, the recovery of the fullness of the good news in the recovery of the heart of the kingdom, the coming of God. From God as the key of the kingdom must emerge "a comprehensive enterprise where the Gospel is shared in depth and out of the depth of man's need and life situations, so that the knowledge of Christ may one day truly cover the earth as the waters cover the sea."[94]

The sovereign grace of His kingdom rule may not be reduced to the traditional Scholastic role of "perfecting nature," understood in its earlier sense "as a divine mystery, operative from within people's lives as the source from which they reach out for truth and justice,"[95] or in its liberation sense as "God's gracious presence to the world as source of transformation and new life."[96] Nor may it be reduced by the traditional evangelical wariness toward social involvement into social irrelevance. The gospel revolution, the life-embracing message of Christ as benevolent dictator still calls for discipleship in "all things whatsoever I command you" (Matt. 28:20), and that may not be reduced to extended hands at foreign missions conference or a program of church growth which intentionally or unintentionally bypasses social and political new creations.

The nerve center of this God-centered contextualization will be praxis. Praxis, the liberation theologians remind us, is that through which "people enter their historical identity. Since praxis changes the world as well as the actors, it becomes the starting point for a clearer vision and a more correct understanding of history. Praxis is the precondition of knowledge. . . ."[97] Liberation theology locates that praxis in the dialectic interaction of reflection and action in the concreteness of history. The evangelical must locate its origin in the triune God. Through His ordering and redemptive intervention people enter their historical identity as the sons of Adam. Since God changes the world as well as the actors, He becomes the starting point not simply for a clearer vision but for the only vision without which the people perish (Prov. 29:18). He is the center for the only correct understanding of history. "He does according to His will in the host of heaven and among the inhabitants of earth; and no one can ward off His hand or say to Him, 'What hast Thou done?' " (Dan. 4:35). Reflection on Him and action flowing "from Him and through Him and to Him" (Rom. 11:36) is the precondition of knowledge. Without the covenantally lived out acknowledgment of God as center of praxis, "Israel does not know, My people do not understand" (Isa. 1:3).

This God-centered praxis is not formed out of dialectic interaction between text and context but from that "dialogue between creator and creature—not an endless back and forth movement, but dialogue which in all its moments has God-given direction and structure and hence in its deepest sense is monologue."[98] It is monologue in which the sovereign suzerain calls for the hermeneutic response of life from man as vassal. "We speak because he has spoken and continues to speak."[99]

This dialogue/monologue must be covenant-framed conscientization. For Paulo Freire, the process of conscience awakening is a pedagogical apparatus that turns from the alphabetization domination and repression to a critical self-awareness of the possibility and means of liberation. The struggle of that awakening is ultimately between being oneself or being in duality, whether to follow prescriptions or to create options, whether to actuate oneself or maintain the illusion that one is being actuated in the action of the oppressors, whether to pronounce the word or not to have a voice, whether to be a mass or a people.[100]

Evangelicals—both North American missionaries and Latin American nationals—respond not with a call for conscientization but for middle class upward mobility, a pedagogical apparatus that turns from the demands of living under the lordship of Jesus Christ in all of life's dimensions to an uncritical self-defense of the status quo.[101] "So concerned are the middle classes with their status that they have erected subtle but effective barriers around themselves and their churches to prevent being mistaken for anything but what they are— middle class, comfortable, and harmless."[102]

A fully God-centered praxis cannot be content with either liberation theology's dialogical action for freedom or the evangelical's respect for the status quo. He must pronounce before and in the world the word authenticated by God. He must call for conscientization that flows from *humanitas* as covenant creature, as image of God (Gen. 1:26) called in covenant to live by covenant before his great King. The covenant task entrusted to man in the garden, God's staked-out covenant terrain (Gen. 2:8-14),[103] a task abandoned by fallen man now under covenant curse, must once again be picked up by man restored to covenant sonship in Christ (Ps. 8:5ff.; Luke 3:38). In Christ, the image of God (II Cor. 4:4; Phil. 2:6; Col. 1:15), man restored to covenant image must turn again to covenant responsibility. The borders of the garden will be extended "to the ends of the earth" (Acts 1:8), and man-as-covenant-responder-to-Covenant-Maker's-demands will find in that task "the glorious libera-

108

tion of the sons of God" (Rom. 8:21).

This covenant conscientization will have a twofold dialogical direction, a critical and growing self-awareness of his restored covenant relationship to Creator as "man of God" (I Tim. 6:11) and a critical and growing self-awareness of his restored covenant relationship to the cosmos. He will be "man as he makes his way through the world, not enclosed in himself, not independent and autonomous but as man of God."[104] The gods of the Hittite vassals—mountains, rivers, springs, the great sea, heaven and earth—will not be covenant witnesses to this conscientization. In God's covenant structure, He who "makes the heaven and the earth" (Gen. 1:1) divests the creation of deity but does not divest them of their roles as covenant witnesses (Deut. 4:26). "Heaven and earth" will be revealing witnesses to the covenant God (Ps. 19:1; 50:6; 89:5; Rom. 1:19-20) of covenant man's calling as stewards of the *politeia* of creation.

Covenant-framed conscientization will not be content with merely "Evangelism-in-Depth" campaigns that close their programs at the end of a year or more of mobilization evangelism. They will call also for "Depth-in-Evangelism" campaigns that close their activities only with the return of Christ, programs as comprehensive as the demands of the day of the new covenant, and the dimensions of the kingdom of God, inaugurated at Christ's first coming and consummated at His second coming. Politics, economics, social life must taste the new order of life initiated by the sovereign rule of God through the death and resurrection of His Son, Jesus Christ. The kingdom as a sign of liberation and of judgment must bring believers to a covenant conscientization of their witnessing responsibility to the demands of the life of the kingdom in every situation.[105]

This covenant conscientization cannot take place without a covenant hermeneutic. For the theology of liberation, hermeneutic is sought on "not primarily the cognitive level of understanding and interpretation, but the *historical* level of praxis and obedience."[106] And for those like Miguez-Bonino, this affirmation is a rejection both "of subjectivism and voluntarism, in which all objective historical contents either in Christianity or of the present are vacated," and for those who would find "an absolute truth, or Christian principles, somehow enshrined in Scripture and/or in the pronouncements of the Church,"[107] it is an affirmation "that there is no truth outside or beyond the concrete historical events in which men are involved as agents. There is, therefore, no knowledge except in action itself, in the process of transforming the world through participation in history."[108] The classical view of truth rejected by Bonino does not correspond, he argues, to the biblical concept of truth in which God's Word is not conceptual communication but a creative event, a history-making pronouncement. Thus truth in the Johannine epistles is not reached through a mere exegetical exercise but through *doing*. Rather, "every interpretation of the texts which is offered to us . . . must be investigated in relation to the praxis out of which it comes."[109] In that investigation, the "suspecting" instruments of men like Freud and Marx "are of great significance."

In response to this criticism, evangelical participation in the con-textualization dialogue has been disappointing. Properly fearful of the judgments such a view makes of the Scripture, the tendency has been simply to repeat the classical view discarded by the liberation theologians. In so doing, we have not seen either the challenge of the contextualization debate or how the processes of enculturation can use even the Reformation principle of *sola Scriptura* to reinforce a reactionary social posture on the part of the churches which seek to adhere to it.[110] "In the face of a contemporary challenge to obey the gospel . . . the supposition that scripture is somehow 'sufficient' to provide the church with whatever answer should be given, coupled with an encultured hesitancy, can lead the interpreter to seek in the Bible answers to questions which are not inherent within the social situation in which the text was written. Insofar as the interpreter finds no answers that speak directly to the current situation he or she finds in such silence warrant for supporting the *status quo* on the question in view, even though the *status quo*, of course, likewise finds no explicit biblical warrant for its policy on the question in hand. The same hermeneutical principle can also work in the oppo-site direction to the detriment of the integrity of the biblical texts. Christians on the 'progressive' or change-advocating side of a con-temporary issue can be so eager to find an answer in the sufficient scripture that models of action suitable to the present can be imposed on the text."[111] Carried far beyond the differences between Calvinist and Lutheran on the "regulative principle of worship," the end result is not simply permission for what the Scripture does not explicitly or by good and necessary consequence deny, but a manipulation of Scripture in favor of what the particular cultural or social point of view of the interpreter can affirm either explicitly or by good and necessary consequence.

We would offer a covenant hermeneutical axiom that the divine word of the covenant has been inscripturated, a divine monologue calling forth man's dialogue response in covenant "for teaching, for reproof, for correction, for training in righteousness" (II Tim. 3:16). We realize this lays us open to Bonino's charges of enshrining absolute truth. But the covenant structure of the hermeneutic demands it be so. The activity of covenant conscientization must have its covenant witnesses. The classic Hittite suzerain treaty patterns by which God constructed His word in apologetic with the cultural world of the Bible made provision for this documentation in the depositing of one copy of the treaty in a sanctuary of the vassal and another in the sanctuary of the suzerain. They were to serve as a witness to the gods of their covenant obligations, sworn before them by the vassal and as a witness to the vassals and the vassal king, and therefore read in their presence each year.[112]

In the organic unfolding of God's covenant of grace with man, that pattern is repeated. The tree of the knowledge of good and evil becomes a witness of the heart of the covenant blessing and the covenant curse, the instrument of man's radical covenant decision. The garden serves as both the sanctuary of the vassal, Adam, and of the suzerain, Jehovah. As eating and drinking was "a recognized symbolic method by which people swore treaties,"[113] so now, noneating is the test of the covenant. For the same reason, the command is given to Moses to write the words of the covenant (Ex. 24:4). In writing the book of the covenant, Moses is continuing the work begun by the finger of God upon the tablets of stone. "The covenantal content of God's revelation requires that this word which has been brought near by revelation should be inscripturated that it might be taught to the people and to their children (Ex. 4:14-16; 24:12; Deut. 5:31). God's instruction out of heaven is written so that it may be taught by Moses, the priests, the prophets, the judges, and the king."[114]

Even the promise of a new covenant does not escape the inscription of covenant witness. Only now it is sealed not by the prophet but by "the scribe of the kingdom," who brings forth from the treasury things new and old, word promised and word fulfilled (Matt. 13:52). The apostolate is commissioned by Christ to link old covenant word with new (Luke 24:44, 45). They are to be witnesses of covenant demands in the new day of the Spirit. So the Book of Acts uses language like "teaching and evangelizing the word of the Lord" repeatedly (Acts 15:35; cf. 13:16-41; 19:8; 20:24f.). In the day of the kingdom, with no tables of stone or ark depository, the word of the covenant is entrusted to the hands of good and faithful men who shall be able to teach (II Tim. 1:14).

It is this very covenant character of hermeneutic that answers liberation theology's concern over the divorce of absolute truth from historical action. For covenant witness is always witness to covenant life before the suzerain and before the world of history. The only deliverance from the covenant curse was unconditional submission to the covenant Maker. So Moses is given a second set of tablets by the Lord after Israel's display of obstinacy and sin. And the Lord's response to his petition for forgiveness and restoration is, "I am going to make a covenant" (Ex. 34:10). So the great reform under Josiah is structured around covenant renewal. And the heart of the covenant is "to walk after the Lord and to keep his commandments and his testimonies and his statutes with all his heart and with all his soul, to carry out the words of this covenant that were written in this book" (II Kings 23:3). So, the word "know" in the prophetic literature borrows its rich background from its covenant usage in Hittite and Akkadian texts where it was used in two technical legal senses: to recognize as legitimate suzerain or vassal, and to recognize treaty stipulations as binding.[115] And Jehovah's rebuke of his people through Amos becomes a covenant curse for obligations unfulfilled. "You only have I known of all the families on earth. Therefore I

112

will punish you for your iniquities" (Amos 3:1-2; cf. Hosea 13:4-5; 4:1-2; Jer. 22:15-16; 24:7). It is precisely against this covenant background that the Johannine injunctions referred to by Bonino find their richest significance.

Such a covenant hermeneutic cannot sacrifice the normative function of Scripture or the demands for covenant response to the Word of the Lord. The covenant authority of the Word of the Great King lays its comprehensive claims upon the total life of the people of God. It will not let us merely profess our allegiance to covenant. It will curse us when we do not walk by covenant in the cultures of the world. The Bible's own understanding of its hermeneutical role in the process of contextualization forbids us the bondage of abstractionism and any culturally privileged status quo. It calls us to the task of the renovation of creation in the name of the last Adam.

Notes

1. Aharon Sapsezian, "Theology of Liberation—Liberation of Theology Educational Perspectives," *Theological Education* IX, 4 (Summer, 1973), 254.
2. *Ibid.,* 257.
3. José Miguez-Bonino, "New Theological Perspectives," *Religious Education* LXVI, 6 (1971), 405.
4. Gustavo Gutiérrez, *A Theology of Liberation* (Maryknoll: Orbis Books, 1973), p. 15.
5. Shoki Coe, "In Search of Renewal in Theological Education," *Theological Education* IX, 4 (Summer, 1973), 237.
6. *Ministry in Context* (Bromley, Kent: Theological Education Fund, 1972), p. 12.
7. Coe, *op. cit.,* 235.
8. *Ibid.,* 236.
9. *Ministry in Context,* pp. 12-13.
10. Coe, *op. cit.,* 237.
11. The tendency in much literature commenting on this shift is to stress the differences between "indigenization" and "contextualization." For examples, see: Coe, *ibid.,* 240-241; Stephen Knapp, "Contextualization and Its Implications for U.S. Evangelical Churches and Missions (unpublished paper, Abington, Pa.; Partnership in Mission, 1976), 5. It may

be better to recognize, with James Berquist, that "contextualization suggests all that is meant by the longstanding concern for indigenization, but perhaps more" ("The TEF and the Uncertain Future of Third World Theological Education," *Theological Education* IX, 4 [Summer, 1973], 251).

12. Max Warren, ed., *To Apply the Gospel: Selections from the Writings of Henry Venn* (Grand Rapids: William B. Eerdmans Publishing Co., 1971), p. 28; Peter Beyerhaus and Henry Lefever, *The Responsible Church and the Foreign Mission* (Grand Rapids: William B. Eerdmans Publishing Co., 1964), pp. 26ff.
13. Warren, *ibid.*, p. 25.
14. Norman Goodall, ed., *Missions Under the Cross* (London: Edinburgh House Press, 1953), pp. 195-196.
15. Coe, *op. cit.*, 240; *Ministry in Context*, p. 20.
16. Coe, *ibid.*, 241.
17. *Ministry in Context*, p. 30.
18. Peter Beyerhaus, *Missions: Which Way?* (Grand Rapids: Zondervan Publishing House, 1971), pp. 35-39.
19. Knapp, *op. cit.*, 5; Peter Beyerhaus, *Bangkok 73* (Grand Rapids: Zondervan Publishing House, 1974), pp. 73-75.
20. *Ministry in Context*, p. 20.
21. Berquist, *op. cit.*, 246.
22. Knapp, *op. cit.*, 3-4.
23. Coe, *op. cit.*, 241.
24. *Loc. cit.*
25. Ministry in Context, p. 20.
26. Coe, *op. cit.*, 238.
27. *Learning in Context* (Bromley, Kent: Theological Education Fund, 1973), p. 14.
28. Knapp, *op. cit.*, 4.
29. José Miguez-Bonino, *Doing Theology in a Revolutionary Situation* (Philadelphia: Fortress Books, 1975), p. 88.
30. Knapp, *op. cit.*, 7.
31. *Ministry in Context*, p. 20.
32. *Ibid.*, pp. 17-18.
33. Sapsezian, *op. cit.*, 262.
34. Paulo Freire, *Pedagogy of the Oppressed* (New York: Herder and Herder, 1971), p. 75.
35. Coe, *op. cit.*, 242.
36. Hugo Assmann, *Practical Theology of Liberation* (London: Search Press Ltd., 1975), p. 104.
37. Coe, *op. cit.*, 241.
38. Rosemary Reuther, *Liberation Theology* (New York: Paulist Press, 1972), p. 178.

114

39. Attention to discontinuity is completely missing from Sapsezian's essay.
40. Victor Nazario, "Theological Education and the Third World: Searching for Fundamental Issues," *Learning in Context*, p. 18.
41. *Ibid.*, p. 21.
42. *Ibid.*, p. 23.
43. *Ibid.*, p. 25.
44. Gutiérrez, *op. cit.*, pp. 22-37; Miguez-Bonino, *op. cit.*, pp. 21-36.
45. J. D. Douglas, ed., *Let the Earth Hear His Voice* (Minneapolis: World Wide Publications, 1975), pp. 1216-1234.
46. *Ibid.*, p. 1217.
47. *Loc. cit.*
48. *Ibid.*, p. 7.
49. Samuel Escobar, "The Development of a Theology That Is Ecumenically Responsible and Culturally Authentic" (unpublished paper, the Second Reformed Missions Consultation, Grand Rapids, Mich., April 12-14, 1976), 1.
50. *Ibid.*, 11-12.
51. René Padilla, "Theology in Latin America," *Theological News Monograph No. 5* (Oct., 1972), 1-5; "Theology in the Making," *Christianity Today* XVIII, 16 (May 10, 1974), 60; *The Contextualization of the Gospel* (Abington, Pa.: Partnership in Mission, 1975), pp. 8-11.
52. Rubem Alvez, *A Theology of Human Hope* (Washington: Corpus Books, 1969), p. i.
53. W. R. Reid, V. M. Monterroso, H. A. Johnson, *Latin American Church Growth* (Grand Rapids: William B. Eerdmans Publishing Co., 1969), p. 351.
54. Emilio Antonio Nuñez, "Contextualization—Latin American Theology," *Latin American Pulse* XL, 2 (Feb., 1976), 6.
55. *Reports of the Annual Mission Executives Retreat, Sept. 29–Oct. 2, 1975* (Washington, D. C.: EFMA, 1975), pp. 53-54.
56. *Ibid.*, p. 54.
57. Nuñez, *op. cit.*, 5.
58. The pioneering work of men like Eugene Nida, William A. Smalley, and William Reyburn and of the journal, *Practical Anthropology*, has been of great service. One waits for the book-length formulations of Charles H. Kraft at Fuller Theological Seminary with much anticipation, whetted by his essays, "Towards a Christian Ethnotheology," in *God, Man and Church Growth*, Alan R. Tippett, ed. (Grand Rapids: William B. Eerdmans Publishing Co., 1973), pp. 109-126, and "Theology and Theologies —Parts I, II, *Theology News and Notes* XVI, 2 (June, 1972), 4-6. 9; XVIII, 3 (Oct., 1972), 17-20.
59. A notable exception to this statement is the initiation of a study task force on the contextualization of the gospel in the eastern United States, in-

115

augurated by the promptings of Partnership in Mission. The first meeting of the group convened on January 29-31, 1976, at Pipersville, Pa.

60. Charles H. Kraft, *Christianity and Culture,* prepublication draft (Pasadena: Fuller Theological Seminary, 1973), pp. 7-8.

61. *Ibid.,* p. 8. Kraft cites as an example of this tendency, the writings of Francis Schaeffer, "whose otherwise extremely perceptive insights and constructive approach to the contemporary scene," he fears, "is marred by the apparent assumption that the only truly Christian approach to the new conceptualization is a desperate flight back into the old" (*ibid.,* pp. 8-9). This may very well be a contributing factor to the lack of sophistication in much of the evangelical discussion we have commented on previously.

62. Eugene Nida's book, *Message and Mission: The Communication of the Christian Faith* (New York: Harper and Brothers, 1960), pp. 221-229, in its attempt to outline a theology of communication, built on the cultural, anthropological model, is not at all clear in its view of the Scripture. His activistic model of the Bible and communication may be judged to show an indebtedness to neo-orthodoxy. How much of that charge is true, and how much is influenced by the controlling concepts of anthropology, is difficult to determine to this author.

63. For the use of this language, compare A. O. Dyson, "Dogmatic or Contextual Theology?," *Study Encounter* VIII, 3 (1972), 1-8.

64. This absence of a biblically oriented apologetic examination of anthropological framework is illustrated in the work of Marvin K. Mayers, *Christianity Confronts Culture* (Grand Rapids: Zondervan Publishing House, 1974). See the book review by Harvie M. Conn, *Christianity Today* XIX, 20 (July 4, 1975), 54-55.

65. There is a desperate need in this whole area for an application of the presuppositional apologetics of Cornelius Van Til to anthropology and the conceptualizations of culture emerging from it.

66. Knapp, *op. cit.,* 10.

67. *Ministry in Context,* p. 30.

68. *Ibid.,* pp. 19-20.

69. Miguez-Bonino, *op. cit.,* pp. 138, 143.

70. Assmann, *op. cit.,* p. 5.

71. *Ministry in Context,* p. 20.

72. Nazario, *op. cit.,* p. 21.

73. *Ibid.,* p. 25.

74. Knapp, *op. cit.,* 12. Knapp says such a view of revelation "does insufficient justice to revelation." We much prefer to say it "undermines" that concept.

75. My language here is quite similar to Knapp, *loc. cit.* However, Knapp draws at this point from A. O. Dyson's argument, *op. cit.,* 6. I find

Dyson's distinction between "dogmatic" and "contextual" theology to be very problematic, in view of his rejection of "dogmatic" theology as a methodology to be discarded in the wake of the acceptance by the twentieth century of liberal historico-critical presuppositions as legitimate (Dyson, *op. cit.*, 3-4). I am confident that Knapp does not accept this background to the distinction either, but the quotation is not helpful for that reason.

76. Gutiérrez, *op. cit.*, p. 262.
77. Knapp, *op. cit.*, 12.
78. Knapp, by way of contrast, notes, "Our disagreement is not so much at the level of analysis as of prescription" (*ibid.*, 14).
79. Knapp, *loc. cit.*
80. Assmann, *op. cit.*, p. 104.
81. Padilla, *op. cit.*, p. 12.
82. Pablo Perez, "Biblical Theology and Cultural Identity in Latin America," *Let the Earth Hear His Voice*, p. 1252.
83. Nuñez, *op. cit.*, 2-3.
84. This is the whole focus of Nuñez, *ibid.*, 5-6. Three of the four suggested definitions offered in the Lausanne study group also concentrated on this dimension. *Let the Earth Hear His Voice*, p. 1226.
85. Knapp's definition does justice to this element when he asserts that "contextualization in the dynamic process through which the church continually challenges and/or incorporates—transforms elements of the cultural and social milieu of which it is an integral part in its daily struggle to be obedient to the Lord Jesus Christ in its life and mission in the world" (*ibid.*, 15).
86. Assmann, *op. cit.*, p. 59.
87. Samuel Escobar, "Evangelism and Man's Search for Freedom, Justice and Fulfillment," *Let the Earth Hear His Voice*, p. 310.
88. Knapp, *op. cit.*, 15.
89. *Loc. cit.*
90. René Padilla's usage of this language is intended precisely to repudiate the notion of speculative theology structured on a Greek methodology for what he calls "functional theology." However, there is to this writer a difficulty in understanding his argument at this point. This may flow from his reluctance to see *any* "system in theology" (a point made by him in reply to the argument of his responder at the time). Padilla's legitimate concern over these questions of methodology needs clarification if he is to avoid the reduction of the importance of "orthodoxy" as a biblically orbed definition shaped and being shaped in the church as a standard to measure overaccommodation (syncretism), unprophetic and inauthentic contextualization, etc. One must set what has been traditionally designated confession of the truth (orthodoxy) into a framework

117

of obedience and discipleship (orthopraxis) without depreciating either the critical place of the practice of the truth as the focus of conscientization or the critical place of the truth which is practiced as the focuser of conscientization.

91. James F. Conway, *Marx and Jesus: Liberation Theology in Latin America* (New York: Carlton Press, Inc., 1973), p. 162.
92. Juan Luis Segundo, *Nuestra Idea de Dios* (Buenos Aires: Ed. Carlos Lohle, 1970), p. 52.
93. Conway, *op. cit.,* p. 156.
94. Orlando Costas, "In-Depth Evangelism in Latin America," *Let the Earth Hear His Voice,* p. 212.
95. Gregory Baum, "The Christian Left at Detroit," *The Ecumenist* 13, 6 (Sept.–Oct., 1975), 82.
96. *Ibid.,* 84.
97. *Ibid.,* 85.
98. Richard B. Gaffin, Jr., "Contemporary Hermeneutics and the Study of the New Testament," *Westminster Theological Journal* XXXI, 2 (May, 1969), 140.
99. *Loc Cit.*
100. Paulo Freire, *Pedagogía del Oprimodo* (Montivideo: Tierra Nueva, 1970), p. 45.
101. Charles H. Troutman, "Evangelicals and the Middle Classes in Latin America—Part 2," *Evangelical Missions Quarterly* 7, 3 (Spring, 1971), 154-156.
102. Roger Greenway, *An Urban Strategy for Latin America* (Grand Rapids: Baker Book House, 1973), p. 119.
103. The care with which Genesis describes the geographical dimensions of the garden of Eden must be seen in the light of the demands of ancient Hittite suzerainty treaties that stated precisely the nature and extent of the land entrusted to the vassal. The vassal, in receiving the land, received also the covenant obligations that went with the land—taxation, military defense, fealty to the Great King (cf. Genesis 23). Compare Klaus Baltzer, *The Covenant Formulary* (Philadelphia: Fortress Press, 1971), p. 12. Thus, the description of the garden becomes part of God's covenant demand now imposed on Adam for covenant response, imposing of covenant responsibility and covenant authority in responsibility.
104. G. C. Berkouwer, *Man: The Image of God* (Grand Rapids: William B. Eerdmans Publishing Co., 1962), pp. 195-196.
105. Orlando Costas, "Depth in Evangelism," *Let the Earth Hear His Voice,* pp. 677-678, 682. As a matter of fact, the structural shift suggested by Costas has taken place within the Latin America Mission that pioneered Evangelism-in-Depth. In 1971, the Institute of In-Depth Evangelism succeeded the former program in an effort to bring greater focus on

Christ's kingdom lordship.
106. Miguez-Bonino, *op. cit.*, p. 87.
107. *Ibid.*, p. 88.
108. *Loc. cit.*
109. *Ibid.*, p. 91.
110. In this connection, the language of Stephen Knapp is somewhat un-
    guarded in his comment that "the *'sola scriptura'* principle inherited from
    the Reformation contributes significantly to a reactionary social pos-
    ture" (*op. cit.*, 34). It is not the principle but its cultural manipulation
    and reduction that is the contributing factor.
111. Knapp, op. cit., 34-35.
112. Delbert R. Hillers, *Covenant: The History of a Biblical Idea* (Baltimore:
    Johns Hopkins Press, 1969), pp. 35ff.
113. Meredith G. Kline, *By Oath Consigned* (Grand Rapids: William B.
    Eerdmans Publishing Co., 1968), p. 16.
114. Edmund P. Clowney, *Preaching and Biblical Authority* (Grand Rapids:
    William B. Eerdmans Publishing Co., 1961), p. 49.
115. Hillers, *op. cit.*, p. 121.

6. Liberation Theology:
Lessons Positive and Negative

KENNETH HAMILTON

My first chapter argued that liberation theology, as a theoretical framework, operates in a thought-world totally opposed to that of biblical Christianity. Liberation theology, however, is not merely a theory. It may even be seen as being primarily an active participation in concrete contemporary events. If it is not a possible version of the Christian gospel, it undoubtedly has a Christian inspiration. It grows out of an element of the gospel which is not only clearly present in the Bible but is almost omnipresent there. This element is compassion for the poor and the downtrodden of this world.

The biblical command in both the Old and the New Testaments is love of the neighbor, especially in his time of need. The person who seeks the merciful God must himself show mercy. When anyone takes his own prosperity to be the sign of God's favor and in consequence isolates himself in proud self-sufficiency, he thereby demonstrates his faithlessness to the God whose righteousness and forgiveness are offered to all His children, however undeserving. In the New Testament, moreover, Jesus is shown to have identified Himself with the outcasts of society and to have declared that salvation was especially extended to those who were neither rich in the world's goods nor in their own esteem.

Liberationists point out that Christian love for the neighbor cannot be shown merely by the rich giving, out of their abundance, alms to the poor. There is a social as well as a personal dimension to Christian charity. And they claim that a true community in Christ is impossible so long as social barriers to that community are not pulled down and brothers and sisters in the faith enjoy an unequal freedom: for some, a "spiritual" freedom solely, for others a freedom to dominate over their brethren. More particularly, it becomes a scandal when the Christian churches form a partnership with the forces of oppression in society, preaching human inequality to be a decree of the divine will and therefore to be accepted in uncomplaining obedience.

I

Liberationists believe that the established dualism in Christian thinking has sundered "spiritual" truths from their incarnation in social realities. This dualism they hope to overcome through what they term *orthopraxis*. The word has been coined with the intention of showing the inadequacy of a mere *orthodoxy*. Orthodoxy regards the Christian life in terms of right thinking, a course which leaves open the choice of being hearers of the Word and not doers—with a consequent blessing being given to hypocrisy. Thought should never be divorced from *praxis,* that is, the practical application of beliefs in concrete action.

Praxis is a term introduced from Marxism (as, for that matter, *liberation* is also). In its practical side as well as in its theoretical side, liberation theology has been developed in association with Marxist revolutionary movements. Liberationists, though, are quick to point out that the association stems from the fact that politically aware Christians and Marxists have a common concern for oppressed peoples. Thus there are areas where cooperation between the two sets of believers is both possible and desirable. It does not follow, so they insist, that liberationists are tied to either the theory or the praxis of Marxist groups of any complexion. Conflicts, indeed, will arise both on an ideological level and on the level of praxis whenever cooperation between Christians and Marxists continues for any time. What the recognition of a common ground between Christian and Marxist social action brings to light is the illegitimacy of the historical link between the established Christian churches and the supporters of the political and economic status quo.

Christianity, say the liberationists, has become the religious ideology of Western capitalism. Thus the Christian gospel, when imported to non-Western nations, has been preached in the context of colonial and imperial rule. Subject peoples have been allowed to appropriate only those elements of the gospel message that pose no threat to the secure title of rulers to perpetuate their domination. The freedom proclaimed in the New Testament has consequently been "spiritualized" in order that oppressed peoples and classes should not question their unfree state but accept it as the God-given order of creation.

To those of us who do not find the Marxist analysis of history convincing, the fact that liberation theology makes this analysis the starting-point for its orthopraxis will be the reason, no doubt, for our vehement rejection of the liberationist position. Yet it is here that liberation theology probably makes its most important contribution to our understanding of the gospel for today. It is not that the liberationist case becomes at this point convincing. It is rather that it seems to us precisely so unconvincing. And thus we are driven to ask ourselves why. Why are we so sure that liberation theology is on the wrong track?

As non-Marxists we are likely to wish to argue with the liberationists about their mistaken views concerning Marxism being the route to freedom. We shall point out that history gives no support to the opinion that Marxist societies bring any real advance in human freedom, for all empirical evidence points to the reverse verdict. Liberal democracy, on the other hand, has demonstrably widened freedom for millions of the earth's inhabitants. Although oppression has by no means vanished from our planet—and never will do so, given human imperfection, outside the wish-fulfilment of an unrealizable utopia—yet actual and solid advances in the restraint of oppression has been achieved in non-Marxist countries. As long as the state is regarded as being both imperfect and reformable, so long may vigilance and effort by free citizens continue to bring about needed reforms.

If we do argue in this vein, then one truth is abundantly clear. This truth is that we have already assumed the end which liberation theology has asserted. We have agreed that the implication of Christian freedom drawn by the liberationists are correct, and we are simply disagreeing over the means by which liberation is to be achieved.

II

In the history of the Christian churches, heresy has always paved the way for a better definition of orthodoxy. I believe that such may prove to be the case today. We are being forced to consider the presuppositions not only of the liberationists but also of those who opposed liberationism. Because liberationists claim so insistently to be correcting a longstanding false development in the history of Christianity (one most usually identified with the Constantinian establishment), they call Christians to look again at the whole question of the relation between the church and the world. Such a reappraisal is assuredly necessary—and, surely, long overdue.

Anti-liberationists accuse liberationists of substituting Marxist ideology for the gospel. But liberationists counter them with the claim that what they call the gospel is, in fact, capitalist ideology. Against the argument that defends the politico-economic theory of progress-through-reform they charge that this theory certainly goes against the evidence of history. The advance in freedom in liberal-democratic societies is no doubt real. Yet it has both its limits and its penalties. The limits are seen at the point where life in the so-called free societies can be maintained only through increasing regimentation and repression. The result is that "freedom" becomes an empty word whose actual content is frustration and hopelessness. The penalties attendant upon the practice of the capitalist ideology are even more manifest. These penalties are inflicted upon those nations upon the exploitation of which the affluence of the so-called free societies depends. In a world in which the gap between the "have" and the "have-not" nations (and between the rich and the poor in every nation) is visibly widening, belief in a theory of progress-through-reform can only be embracing an illusion.

Now, the question as to which of the two ideological arguments is superior can be debated. Liberationists will claim that history is quickly resolving the debate. The oppressed nations are opting for Marxism, in one form or another—they know what oppression means and where liberation is to be found. Anti-liberationists will say that the historical process is far less simple. The gains of Marxism are to be explained by the infatuation of intellectuals with Marxist theory and by the ability of these intellectuals to exploit the just grievances of the uneducated. The fact that world Marxism is now divided into factions more preoccupied with consolidating their individual power-complexes than with advancing the Marxist dream of a liberated humanity proves that the dream was always an illusion. Meanwhile, the so-called liberated peoples are finding that they are less free than they were before their liberation. The People's Democracies are experiencing all the age-old oppressions known to history as the rule of tyranny and arbitrary power.

In the world of politics the result of this debate is still undecided; and for that world the result will be completely crucial. It is hardly surprising that Christians should be drawn into the debate and be found as ardent advocates for one side or the other. Yet, can it be for them completely crucial? Is not the one thing crucial for Christians the cross of Christ? Is not the gospel the message of the salvation brought about through the cross—and, therefore, the freedom with which Christ has made us free no matter what the political situation under which we live? Did the Constantinian establishment decisively rob Christians of this freedom? And can it be that either the continuance of liberal democracy or the triumph of one or the other of the varieties of Marxist revolution will restore to us the essence of Christian freedom?

These and similar questions are the ones which the advent of liberation theology forces us to ask. Without the challenge of liberationist versions of Christian faith we should not have stopped to ask them—or, at least, to ask them so urgently. And that we can hardly avoid raising these questions at the present juncture of the church's history seems (to me, at least) something of great gain. Heresy is forcing us to re-examine the meaning of orthodoxy.

III

That liberation theology is a heresy I believe to be beyond question, as I have explained in my first chapter. Anyone can examine the strange aberrations of belief to be found in even a "moderate" liberationist view by reading through the document issued as "The Boston Affirmations." Or he can turn to Robert McAfee Brown's keynote address at the W.C.C. General Assembly at Nairobi, where Brown identifies the chief oppressions in the world today as "racism, sexism, classism and imperialism"—not a word being said about nationalism, terrorism, anti-semitism, or totalitarianism and the police state.

Yet liberation theology, though it gives many highly suspect answers, raises some highly pertinent questions. There is, for example, the question of "spiritualizing" the gospel so that political issues are never raised. Liberationists are constantly reminding us that we cannot remain politically neutral and still inhabit a politically organized world. If we try to do so, they tell us, we are taking sides just the same—we are opting for the status quo. We are casting our votes against revolution and for the forces of reaction. Here the liberationists are right—at any rate on the impossibility of political neutrality. The question is not whether Christians are to be involved, either actively or passively, in political decisions. The question is *how, where,* and *in what spirit* their involvement is to be made effective. Yet the options are by no means so clear-cut as liberationists imagine. The Christian choice is not, for example, the one simplistically presented by Robert McAfee Brown prior to Nairobi. Brown suggests that we must choose between being against the Christ whose people are the poor and the oppressed ("those whom our social structures stifle and strangle and suffocate") and "converted" to struggle against all economic and political oppression.

Take the matter of Christians supporting the status quo, to begin with. Of all church bodies adopting this stance, the most consistently subservient to the ruling power is the Russian Orthodox Church— where the status quo is Marxist. This Church has accepted the state ban upon proselytizing, upon public religious observances, and upon religious education. It supports the state in all that relates to the national life; and it raises no protest against state oppression of groups or individuals. Its teaching, so it insists, is wholly spiritual. What we then must ask the liberationists (and ourselves) is this:

Does a Christian body die when it surrenders the right to decide for itself upon matters of liberty in the world, retreating into a "spiritualized" view of what constitutes the Christian faith? And the answer must be "No!" Certainly, a church must be weakened in its witness whenever it ceases to say under any conditions, "We must obey God rather than men." Nevertheless, unless Caesar actually forbids the preaching of the "spiritual" gospel and demands the proclamation of "another gospel," it is impossible to say categorically that Caesar must be opposed. Decisions about civil disobedience or actual support for political measures to dethrone Caesar then become matters for the individual Christian conscience. That is why, when Christians enter politics, they may well find themselves on opposite political sides.

IV

Johannes Metz, one of the leading Roman Catholic theorists of liberationism, has called for a "deprivatizing" of Christian faith. Personally, I would agree with that call; but only if it were joined with an equally loud call to "depoliticize" faith. Christianity involves the whole human being: body, soul, and spirit. It is not for the isolated individual, and neither is it for "the political animal." In his book, *Jesus Means Freedom,* Ernst Käsemann denies that Jesus ever said, "My kingdom is not of this world." Yet, even if we follow Käsemann, it makes little difference in the political context, for Jesus identifies political power with this age, whose ruler is Satan. Our hope as Christians is not in this age, past, present, or to come—even if some like to rename the period of this age still not visible to our senses "the future of God." The announcement of the coming kingdom by Jesus held no hope of this age turning itself inside out in order to emerge as God's kingdom instead of Satan's. Instead he asked the question of his disciples, "When the Son of man shall come, shall he find faith on the earth?"

The duty of Christians is to live with that word in their minds and on their conscience. Compassion for the oppressed will lead them

126

into political action, frequently, as well as constantly requiring them to personal service for the relief of suffering. But they will never put any final trust in politics, remembering that Caesar, while he may protect the weak from the strong to some extent, must always be also an oppressor. Final liberation can be only the resurrection to eternal life. The freedom of the Christian is to be free for faith in faith, knowing that all things work together for good with those who are called according to the purpose of God, which is to free the universe from its present bondage.

7. A Call for the Liberation of North American Christians

CLARK H. PINNOCK*

Because we must hear and obey the Word of God in a specific context, many Christians are seriously asking after the divine command for them in a world largely poor and hungry. A "theology of liberation" is in the air. Latin American and Black theologians are pressing for a radical understanding of what it means to *do* the truth in a situation of oppression and suffering. We dare not, as Hugo Assmann has warned us, reduce their efforts to a new toy on the theological playground of the affluent, Western thinkers. Instead we are summoned to enter into the same struggle, to hear the Word of God ourselves in a world of poverty and dire distress. Evangelicals have in recent years been rather more inclined to *defend* the gospel than to *practice* it. Yet a defending of the gospel which is not matched by a living of it is hollow and ungenuine. The "theology of liberation" is in reality God's instrument for the refinement of our own commitment to the gospel, and has been leading many to reflect on the need for the liberation of North American Christians.

Theological Groundwork

Before issuing such a call, there is a theological assumption to be stated and accepted. All believers in Jesus Christ have been summoned to a life of radical discipleship, oriented to his cross (Mark

---

* Clark H. Pinnock, Ph.D., currently serves on the staff of Regent College as Associate Professor of Systematic Theology. He came to that post after teaching assignments at the New Orleans Baptist Theological Seminary and Trinity Evangelical Divinity School. With a long-term interest in questions revolving around the inspiration and authority of Scripture, he has been a popular speaker at college campuses on areas of apologetic concerns. He is author of such titles as *Set Forth Your Case* and *Biblical Revelation*.

128

8:34). Although the point is familiar and obvious, grounded in the most certain and lucid commands of our Lord himself, it is here that many of us have become stalled. We do not wish to think that the gospel might have radical, life-changing implications for the entire range of our existence. Nevertheless, according to the New Testament, it most certainly does. Paul describes the "reasonable" service of the believer in Jesus in terms of the presenting of our bodies to God as a living sacrifice (Rom. 12:1). Such a metaphor can only be termed "radical," calling as it does for a total, unreserved commitment of the whole life to God. We are invited to respond to Christ on no other terms than these.

Furthermore, the general shape of our discipleship also is made unmistakably clear as an orientation to the cross of Jesus, a life patterned in accordance to the normative event of the gospel. In the cross, as Peter says, Christ has left us an example that we should follow in His steps (I Pet. 2:21). Because He was among us as one who serves, we are to be present in the world after the manner of servanthood. The presence of a community following this rule is, according to Jesus, a primary mark and sign of the truth of the gospel and the coming of the kingdom of God, a city on a hill which cannot be hidden, the pilot project of an entirely new order. The call for the liberation of North American Christians is based on the well-founded assumption that radical discipleship in the mode of servant-hood is a primary demand of the gospel. It is so plainly scriptural that it scarcely can be denied in principle.

The Context of Our Obedience

Christian discipleship in this mode does not take place in a vacuum. It has to be fleshed out in the particular cultural setting where we are, in relation to a critical reflection on our social, political, and personal situation, in which we are expected to act responsibly before God. Just as our Lord in the incarnation identified with the needs and condition of people in His day, so we are sent to shine as lights in the world of our day, addressing its central concerns as we proclaim good news.

As soon as anyone undertakes to analyze the worldly context in

129

which we live, personal assumptions and perceptions rise swiftly to the surface to influence the mental image. Nevertheless, such a judgment has to be made, and on the particulars of which I am thinking there is already widespread agreement. The global context of discipleship is simply grim, and beset with crises, on a colossal scale. We are being reminded from every quarter of the awful disparities in wealth between nations, of the enormous investments in deadly armaments, and of the frantic consumption and irresponsible pollution of the earth's limited resources. The North American context, on the other hand, in relation to the global one, sees itself as a safety island, unaffected by these harsh realities, and largely indifferent to cries for help issuing from the Third World. One need not be an economist or ecologist to sense the enormity of the world's crises, nor an ethical philosopher or theologian to feel shame and outrage at the moral callousness involved in our collective North American behavior. Let us consider two items.

Item One: No Mercy

North Americans—and Christians are not an outstanding exception—are continuing to consume the products of earth at indefensively high rates and appear to be firmly set on reaching even higher levels, at the very time when it is a matter of public record that unaccounted millions are seriously malnourished and even starving. To put it most mildly, we are insensitive to the cries of the world's poor. Like the rich man with Lazarus at his gate, we are largely indifferent to the distress of the needy. Like ancient Sodom, we "have surfeit of the food and prosperous ease, but do not aid the poor and needy" (Ezek. 16:49). Of course humanitarian aid has not been wholly lacking. Mission and relief agencies in particular have faithfully tried to channel funds to needy situations. Even the U.S. and Canada have been active in aid to the poor countries. But it should be recognized that, although these gestures are good, the effort hitherto has been meager and half-hearted. A serious attempt to assist the world's poor has not been made except by a very few, and we stand condemned as pretty largely indifferent to the problem. How then do we suppose we shall escape the wrath of God, we who hold down the truth in unrighteousness? God's Word warns us: "He who closes his ear to the cry of the poor will himself cry out and not be heard" (Prov. 21:13). How can we deny that the attitude of North Americans in general is callous, pleasure seeking, and hardhearted in the face of the world situation? Are we not behaving in a merciless manner that is both globally irresponsible and morally depraved?

Item Two: No Justice

As if that were not enough, to this relative absence of tender-heartedness must be added a shocking lack of justice and fair play. The fact that we control a disproportionately large share of the world's real wealth is partly due to our domination of "world trade," a new economic colonialism by which we have repatriated large profits from countries which have only some basic raw material to sell and a large supply of cheap labor. In every way they are disadvantaged in relation to our superior economic leverage and technical development. We are rather like the fat sheep in Ezekiel's pathetic picture which "push and thrust at the weak until they are scattered abroad" (Ezek. 34:21). We, the wealthy six percent of the earth's population, cluster around the well of the earth's resources and drink deeply from it, while the vast majority of peoples are shunted aside lapping up the trickles that spill from our cups.

Why do we act in this way? What can account for such behavior? Suppose a visitor arrived from outer space and discovered a small group of people feasting on abundance while the majority was in need; found them pursuing policies which drove the poor deeper into despair; and saw them refusing to accept even a slight lowering of their standard of living out of considerations of mercy and of justice. What would he think? Surely he could only conclude that this small but favored minority was in a condition of bondage to the godlike power of materialism and comfort over them, which had closed their hearts and minds to the most elementary demands of justice and mercy. Although God's Word is unequivocally clear in such matters, it would seem that "the cares of the world, the delight in riches, and the desire for other things have entered in, and choked the Word so that it proves unfruitful" (Mark 4:19). The Word of God is choked

131

in the churches of North America. Our comfortable life and culture have blinded our eyes to the scriptural teaching about tenderheartedness, stewardship, and justice. I see no way to deny, though I wish it were not so, that the context in which the Bible is to be responsibly read and applied today is that of a suffering and poor world, containing a small pocket of affluence, in which the privileged, among whom are to be counted most North American Christians, are largely indifferent to the hungry millions at their gate. If the Bible is to be believed, and if this situation is not changed by the costly repentance of these favored few, all we can expect is the wrath and indignation of the God who regards the needy and hears their cry. Where is there mercy and justice amongst us?

Liberation from Bondage to Mammon

I am convinced that God does not desire to pour out his wrath on the peoples of North America, but wants his church as a significant remnant on this continent to experience liberation from bondage to Mammon and enter into lives of credible and costly discipleship. In order to spell out some of the implications of this liberation, we will consider what it may mean to us as individuals, as congregations, and even as nations, to obey God's command to us today.

Liberation as It Applies to Us Individually

Although we can think globally, we can really act only locally. The watchword has to be downward mobility. The per capita consumption in the West measured against the limited resources of spaceship earth and when placed into relation with world poverty, is obviously too high. Our lifestyles must be simplified, and our consumption scaled down. In line with the "Macedonian example" which Paul related to the Corinthian church (II Cor. 8–9), we must begin to share goods in a way that cuts into our standard of living, so that the voluntary self-impoverishment of Jesus may be fleshed out among us, and there may be a semblance of "equality" created. It is simply a matter first of tenderheartedness: how can we live affluently with the eyes of the poor upon us? and secondly, a matter of justice: what gives us the right to accept the privileged position of the world's upper classes consuming far beyond our fair share and as a result accentuat-

132

ing the desperate plight of the poor? "Downward mobility" has nothing to do with asceticism, which despises comfort, good food, and adequate shelter. These things are good, and we wish they were the lot of every man. Life cannot be fully human without a satisfactory physical base beneath it. But an overabundance of these things in a world where our excess is confronted by extreme want is not good or right.

I believe that God is calling North American Christians to a life which is simpler—simpler in diet, in housing, in entertainment, and so forth—a life that celebrates God's jubilee, his good news for the poor and a righting of economic wrongs. Let us accept for ourselves the spartan life which we have asked missionaries to live in our stead in the past, and incorporate into our evangelical spirituality dimensions of practical mercy, simplicity, and justice. Jesus promised that those who lose their lives in costly discipleship will find them again. It belongs to the paradox and irony of the gospel that precisely this commitment to a simpler way results in a full and a better life in the end. Against the Madison Avenue lie, Jesus said pointedly, "A man's life does not consist in the abundance of his possessions." God is calling us as individual believers to test the truth of these words in our day. How else can a Christian be said to carry the cross in a hungry world?

Liberation as It Applies to Us as Congregations

To be a Christian at all is to have been joined by the Spirit to the body of Christ, a fellowship in the context of which the tender plant of our individual Christian freedom is to be nurtured, challenged, and directed. It is very difficult for an individual believer to be radical in his obedience if his congregation or fellowship circle remains indifferent and complacent. The anemic commitment of local congregations in North America to issues of human need and social justice is most discouraging. Instead of being seedbeds nurturing prophetic concerns, they have become safety islands from which these concerns are often excluded. And all this is paralleled ironically by a considerable interest in "church growth." Surely the mere numerical growth of congregations, if it is resulting in the proliferation of

133

pseudo-disciples who can hardly distinguish the cross from the flag, is a very mixed blessing. The "church growth" most urgently needed in North America is growth in the knowledge of the biblical God, who loves justice and mercy, and who calls us all without exception to costly discipleship. We are most definitely in favor of quantitative evangelization and are opposed to its being substituted by or changed into the struggle for social justice. But what we must insist on is a radicalizing of evangelism so that it is more than an individualistic and spiritualistic exercise and involves calling people to accept the full and undiminished lordship of Jesus.

The New Testament congregations nurtured people in radical discipleship. They shared with each other so that economic needs were met, and practiced spiritual gifts that led them to feed and house those who were hungry and homeless. When the Spirit first fell, their economic thinking was so radicalized that they sold their possessions, pooled their resources, and moved in the direction of a social order in which there was justice and equality. Since that time there have been some sterling examples in the experience of the churches where God's people have ventured out in faith, risked their own comfortable security, and expended themselves in Jesus' name on behalf of the needy. Let us build up congregations that proclaim the jubilee of God's justice, that stand for the ongoing servant presence of Jesus in the world, that cross over the road and stand by the needy neighbor in his plight. Until we move in this direction, we are not really loving God and the neighbor as Jesus commanded us. Judgment begins with the people of God. We are being weighed in the balances. God is inspecting the vineyard which he planted to see what fruit is yielding. It is time for all of us in our congregations to take stock, and bring our priorities into line with the stated purposes of God for the church.

Jesus has called his church to be a servant people ministering to all the needs of mankind. Much progress in social history has come about through the impact of radical biblical ideas upon the human spirit. Yet, sadly, as we have become successful and established, we have come to identify with the interests of the ruling classes and the established order, producing bourgeois Christianity, a church no longer willing to care for the needy and hear their cry. Against such a church both God and man will arise in protest and disgust. Let us repent and return to our radical roots.

Liberation as It Applies to Our Nations, the United States and Canada

All Christians can agree that God's Word contains principles that are politically relevant, and need to be injected into present day discussions and decision making. I will list three of them: stewardship, neighborliness, and justice. First, since God has given the earth to all peoples as a sacred trust, it follows that no group has the right to exhaust the earth's limited resources in a lifestyle of unbridled consumption and as a result severely pollute the creation because of their insatiable greed. We must call for a global ethic based on the creational principle of stewardship. It is not enough to ask what will benefit our country. We must also ask what is just and right from a global perspective. Second, because God has made mankind of one stock, in personal relationship and mutual interdependence one with another, it follows that no group has a right to live in a wasteful and selfish way while huge numbers of their fellowmen lack even the basic elements of a decent standard of living. We have no right, for example, to feed huge quantities of our grain to cattle at the very time when millions perish for want of bread. People born into God's world have an inalienable right to eat, and it is a basic ethical obligation of ours to secure that right for them if we can. Third, in terms of justice, it is simply intolerable that six percent of the human race should have a corner on seventy percent of the world's real wealth. A "new international economic order" is essential as a matter of fairness. So long as the desire for profit motivates the world economic system, the needs of the poor cannot be met. Such a system serves only those who can command resources and enter into the market as purchasers. We have come to the point where, in the name of simple justice, human need must be put before profit, and resources must be shifted from wasteful, destructive projects into human development. Barbara Ward estimates that only one-half of the world's annual expenditures on armaments ($100 billion) would fund all the works of mercy and peace for an entire decade and result in significantly alleviating all of the major problems presently obstructing the

135

prospect of a decent kind of life for the world's peoples. With such self-righteousness we look down on the minority of White settlers in Rhodesia, and we wonder what stops them from sharing the blessings of a well-endowed country with their Black majority. Why don't they move toward a social order which would be fairer and in every way wiser even from the viewpoint of simple survival, we ask. But we really need not wonder about it when we in North America are every bit as reluctant to give up our position of affluence on behalf of the hungry billions, and seem as intent as they are on global suicide rather than facing the awful prospect of justice. Nevertheless, it is no exaggeration to say that if we refuse to face up to global injustice today, tomorrow's world is likely to be horrible and violent beyond imagination.

The Bible offers politically relevant criteria that need to be injected into the processes of planning and governing. God is calling for political obedience. For the first time in history, the necessities of the situation and the obligations of the gospel practically coincide. Loving the neighbor has never before been so much a matter of political common sense. It is a time of God's testing. The handwriting is on the wall. The words of the prophets are on the subway walls. Let us arise and seek God's kingdom and his justice.

Conclusion

Evangelicals of late have been more inclined to defend the gospel than to do it. Before us there is a costly decision: whether to break with the false god Mammon and follow after Jesus, or to go back and turn aside because we have great possessions. Jesus said it was hard for the "haves" to enter the kingdom of God because of the demands the gospel makes upon them. False gods do not give up their captives without a struggle. We wrestle not against flesh and blood but against the fallen powers of darkness. Liberation will come only through the miracle working activity of the Spirit of God in our lives. But if that is what we want, and if we are willing to repent and really change at deep levels, then we can experience liberation. We are being weighed in the balances. Will we be faithful and wise stewards pursuing the will of the Lord, or faithless, disobedient servants who will in the end be punished and placed with the unbelievers?